# Negotiating

D0032217

## PHIL BAGULEY

**TEACH YOURSELF BOOKS**

For UK order queries: please contact Bookpoint Ltd, 78 Milton Park, Abingdon, Oxon OX14 4TD. Telephone: (44) 01235 400414, Fax: (44) 01235 400454. Lines are open from 9.00–6.00, Monday to Saturday, with a 24 hour message answering service. Email address: orders@bookpoint.co.uk

For USA & Canada order queries: please contact NTC/Contemporary Publishing, 4255 West Touhy Avenue, Lincolnwood, Illinois 60646–1975, USA. Telephone: (847) 679 5500, Fax: (847) 679 2494.

Long renowned as the authoritative source for self-guided learning – with more than 40 million copies sold worldwide – the *Teach Yourself* series includes over 200 titles in the fields of languages, crafts, hobbies, business and education.

A catalogue record for this title is available from The British Library.

*Library of Congress Catalog Card Number:* On file

First published in UK 2000 by Hodder Headline Plc, 338 Euston Road, London, NW1 3BH.

First published in US 2000 by NTC/Contemporary Publishing, 4255 West Touhy Avenue, Lincolnwood (Chicago), Illinois 60646–1975 USA.

The 'Teach Yourself' name and logo are registered trade marks of Hodder & Stoughton Ltd.

Typeset by Transet Limited, Coventry, England.
Printed in Great Britain for Hodder & Stoughton Educational, a division of Hodder Headline Plc, 338 Euston Road, London NW1 3BH by Cox & Wyman Ltd, Reading, Berkshire.

Impression number    10 9 8 7 6 5 4 3 2
Year                 2005 2004 2003 2002 2001 2000

# CONTENTS

# ACKNOWLEDGEMENTS

Much of what you and I learn in life pivots around the success –
and failure – of our negotiations. Because of this it would be wrong
of me not to acknowledge the contributions made by many of the
people with whom I've negotiated over the years. The list of their
names would be far too long to be published here. However,
acknowledgement must be made of the particular contributions of
my late father-in-law Gilbert Fox and my partner Linda Baguley –
both of whom extended the learning curve of my negotiating – and
hence this book. Thanks also are due to Joanne Osborn, Jill Birch
and Valerie Bingham, all of whom played a role in the journey that
this book made from idea to text.

Phil Baguley
Brighton, England
philb@pavilion.co.uk
Spring 2000

# BEFORE YOU BEGIN . . .

We are all negotiators. Some of us do it well. We get what we want and for a price that's less than we might have been prepared to settle for. Others of us do it badly. We find ourselves giving up something we valued – for less than we had thought it was worth. These negotiations can be about anything – our salaries or wages, the price we pay or get for a house or a car, the cost of a service, the value of our holidays or our computer, who has the family car today, who gets the coffee at work or who pays for the next round of drinks in the bar or pub. We even, so some tell us, negotiate about love and affection.

These negotiations start when we see that someone else has something that we want. But just wanting it isn't enough. For if our negotiations are to be successful we have to be prepared to give up something we value in exchange for it. The climax of these negotiations comes when we and the other side agree to – and then implement – that exchange.

How we get to that exchange is never straightforward or simple. Most of us muddle through; we fall into success by accident rather than by design. Even when we achieve that success we often remain unsure as to whether the other side would have given us more or whether we had given them too much.

The aim of this book is to reduce that uncertainty. Its intention is to give you, its reader, a basic, yet comprehensive, introduction to the process of negotiation. Many – but not all – of you will work in organizations, organizations in which the negotiations that take place range from the formal set-pieces of annual wage reviews to informal debates about whose turn it is to get the Friday afternoon cakes or doughnuts. Others of you will find your negotiating skills challenged by the cut and thrust of family life or the push and pull of the market.

All of you will want to be able to negotiate well. This book will help you to achieve that goal. It will tell you, in an accessible and easily understood form, about:

- the 'hows' and 'whys' of your negotiations
- how you can successfully prepare for and complete those negotiations
- the skills you need to ensure your negotiations succeed.

It starts with a single introductory chapter and is completed by a Further Reading section containing listings of books and web sites which provide further detailed material on a number of aspects of negotiation. Between these are four parts, each of which contains clear, concise and jargon-free material on:

- Preparing for your negotiation
- Carrying out your negotiation
- Completing your negotiation
- Reflections on you and your negotiation.

But this isn't a book to be read once and then cast aside. It is a book to be used again, referred to and browsed over, a book that you, the reader, will continue to use as your negotiating experience and skills grow. It's a book to make *you* a better negotiator.

# 1 | NEGOTIATING AND YOU

*Let us never negotiate out of fear. But let us never fear to negotiate.*

**John F. Kennedy**

Walk into to any office and ask the people working there if they're negotiators. My guess is that the answer you'll get will be 'no'. 'After all', they'll say, 'we aren't involved in wage or contract or purchasing negotiations, the Boss looks after that stuff.' In large organizations the answer you get might be that negotiations are looked after by the Personnel Department or the Industrial Relations or Purchasing Departments. Now try the same thing at home – again, my guess is that you'll get the same sort of answer. But is this true – is negotiation such a specialist activity, only done by a few chosen people? The answer is a loud and unmistakable 'NO'.

For we are all negotiators. We learn the languages of bargain and barter at our mother's knee and we go on to use them throughout the rest of our lives. We negotiate with everyone – bosses, partners, children, friends, enemies, co-workers, suppliers, contractors and customers. There are no exceptions. These negotiations can be about anything and everything – how much we get paid, how much we pay someone else, who is in charge, who decides what, how we get the information, money, goods, resources, and services that we want. Some of these negotiations are formal. They take place in the meeting rooms and board rooms of our office blocks; they are public or organizational events, involving teams of negotiators, rather than single individuals, and drawing on complex systems of rules and relationships. However, most of our negotiations are informal. They take place between us as individuals – at the coffee machine or the water fountain, over the lunch table or the desk, in the market place or street market and in the living rooms and kitchens of our homes. They occur on a day-to-day, hour-by-hour basis; they are about who will do what, when it gets done and, sometimes, why it needs to be done.

The aim of this book is to give you the chance to enhance and extend your ability to undertake these negotiations, to become a skilled negotiator – one who hits his or her target every time. The benefits of doing this are considerable. For effective negotiation is *the* ultimate transferable skill. It can change the way you do your job, the way you manage your career, the way you buy your new car and the way you shop in the market. In short, it can change your life.

## Wants and needs

Wanting is a very human condition. Most of the time this happens because we all, as human beings, have strong drives. These drives are often expressed in our need to achieve goals, goals that are about having our needs answered. We feel that we need to be richer, happier, more successful, more fulfilled.

One of the more accessible views about these needs and drives is that of Abraham Maslow. In his view, we exist in a state of constant and incessant need. These needs, Maslow tells us, are never fully satisfied, and it is this state of 'un-satisfaction' that drives us to act in the ways that we do. Maslow divided our needs into five basic groups. These can be seen as being stacked on top of each other – as in a staircase – with the highest priority needs at the bottom. The first and most basic of these are our physical needs: for food, warmth and shelter. Above these are our needs for protection and security and then, our affection and attachment needs. As we rise further up this 'staircase' we find our needs for reputation and recognition, and above these, at the top, is our need for self-fulfilment. These groups of needs are said to act upon us in their order on the 'staircase'. For example, we have to first satisfy our basic need for warmth, food, water and shelter before we begin to seek answers to our 'higher' needs such as job security, prestige and the freedom to create. However, this is not a totally rigid staircase and there are, as Maslow pointed out to us, people for whom self-esteem is more important than love or for whom the fulfilment of their creative needs overrides all other needs. However, whatever their order, you'll know from your own experience that these needs are at their most potent when they are totally unsatisfied.

So, how does all of this lead to or influence your negotiations? The answer lies in the fact that, most of the time, you and I are unable to answer these needs from our own resources. Because of this, we search to answer them from elsewhere. This involves us in competition with other people. It is this competition that leads us, first, into conflict and then, in seeking an answer to that conflict, into negotiation.

## Conflict, conflict and conflict

Psychologists tell us that being in conflict is a very common experience for all of us. Conflict raises its head whenever and wherever our individual vested interests or desires collide with those of others. Our lives are full of conflicts of one sort or another, conflicts that arise when we compete with others to get what we want. When this sort of competition occurs, one person's behaviour – yours or mine – frustrates someone else getting what they want. We behave in this way because we want to satisfy our needs, as does the other person involved. We can see a simple example of this if we imagine that you and I are driving our cars in opposite directions down a narrow country lane. When we – or rather our cars – meet, both of us will be frustrated. Neither of us will be able to proceed forward because the other car is blocking our way. Our individual sets of needs and goals are in direct opposition to each other. Yet the solution is obvious: one of us must reverse back to the next place at which passing is possible and allow the other to pass. But if neither of us is willing to do this, then we have a conflict situation.

## SHALL WE OR SHAN'T WE?

Sue, the Production Manager, had just got into her office on Monday morning when the phone rang. It was Dave, the Sales Manager. Could she please change the production schedule for this week to squeeze in an order for a 'special customer'? 'It's only a little one,' said Dave. Sue sighed – Dave was always pulling stunts like this. The more she thought about it the more she realized it wasn't a 'little one'. It involved changing equipment set-ups, draining, cleaning and refilling paint dip tanks etc., etc. What should she do? If she gave in she wouldn't meet her production target, if she said 'no' then Dave would lose a sale.

Conflicts like the one above are pretty common in the workplace. Their influence is considerable. They influence the ways that we speak, write, act, feel about and behave towards each other. Often, the feelings and desires we have – about getting or not getting what we want – run high. The results of all this can be pretty destructive; previously good relations can turn sour. This sort of conflict can occur between almost anyone in a workplace. Individuals, teams, departments, sections and even organizations get drawn into it. It can be about the use or possession of scarce resources, such as money or skilled personnel, or about power and influence, such as which individual or department is 'top-dog' when it comes to making decisions about the organization's future. It can also have its roots in our individual likes, dislikes and prejudices.

The organizations in which we work are often seen as 'hotbeds' of conflict; conflicts that often come about as a result of disagreements about the who, why and when of resource control. But this conflict isn't necessarily destructive. Indeed, it can act rather like a forest fire and be a necessary ingredient in the cycle of growth and renewal. Nevertheless, for many of you who work in organizations, life is rich in conflict situations. It is commonplace to be in a situation in which co-workers, other managers, suppliers, customers, employees or trade unions won't or can't back up – or down. Later in this book you'll see that effective communication can make a considerable difference as to whether or not these situations are resolved. But, for now, let's accept that conflict, in one form or another, is present in all our working lives. What we now need to look at is how you can resolve these conflicts.

# Resolving conflict – the choices

The variety of these conflicts is enormous. They can be about almost anything and can involve almost anyone you meet, work, play or live with. Resolving them can make considerable demands upon your time and patience. Given all of this, you shouldn't be too surprised to find that there isn't a single 'right' way of coping with or managing all of these conflicts. You have to make a choice; a choice from a number of ways by which you can manage your conflict. But these ways of conflict management do have a common objective. That is that they enable you either:

■ to resolve your conflict, or

■ to limit its effects or consequences.

This choice about *how* you resolve your conflict will be made by you from the Five Basic Ways of Conflict Management. Let's look at them in more detail so that you can see what they involve.

## Avoiding the conflict

This, the first of the Five Basics, is called the Avoidance style of conflict management. It is often described as being the 'Ignore it and it'll go away' style or, alternatively – and in an industrial relations situation – it's described as the 'Put it into procedure' style. When you use this you limit, or at least try to limit, the effects of conflict by ignoring it. You literally turn your back on it and hope that it will 'go away'. Not a style of conflict management to be used with major conflicts, it does have uses with conflicts that are trivial or have low priorities. You can also use it with conflicts whose cost of resolution outweighs their benefits or those conflicts which you can't, however hard you try, resolve.

## Competing

The Competition style of conflict management is a straightforward and obvious style. It's about making sure that you win and, of course, making just as sure that the other person, department or organization loses. Often called, for obvious reasons, the 'win–lose' style, it uses and exploits power and rivalry; its advocates say 'We take no hostages'. It's a style that, in the heat of battle, can be appealing. But you should always remember that, next time you meet, your opponent will be better prepared, and you could then find yourself on the losing side. It's a disruptive style of conflict management and should generally only be used in emergencies or on unpopular issues. But it does have its uses as, for example, a defensive response when others seek to exploit what they see as your apparent lack of competitiveness.

## Giving in

The third of the Five Basics is the Accommodation style of conflict management. When you use this style you accommodate the needs of others by giving in, by surrendering. For that reason it's often called 'Submit and Comply' style. It's a style that is best used when you find that your conflict is creating major and insuperable difficulties – when you are, almost literally, 'up the creek and without a paddle'. It's also worth using if you find, partway into the conflict, that you're in the wrong or when you need to minimize losses when you're in the right, but losing. The Accommodation style can be useful when you need to reduce the overall level of conflict or to 'restore the peace', and when the conflicts you're involved in have trivial consequences or costs.

## Working together

The fourth of the Five basics is called the Collaboration style of conflict management. When you use this style, which is often described as a 'win–win' style, your objective is to defuse conflict by generating a consensus solution to which all are committed. This often takes a lot of time and demands considerable commitment from both sides. But its potential to restore long-term relationships, by 'working through' feelings, can make it worthwhile. The time it consumes means that it is often only used in major conflict situations or to support relationships that are needed in the long term. Outside our workplaces it forms the core of many relationship counselling processes.

## Finding the middle way

This, the last of our Five Basics, is known as the Compromise style of conflict management. It is about deals and trade-offs. In its broadest form, it is a style that is used to resolve the conflicts created by incompatible goals and to generate appropriate solutions when under time pressure. It is a very effective alternative to the Competition and Collaboration styles – particularly when these would be, respectively, too disruptive or too demanding. The sorts of activity that go on when we use this style are often called 'politicking' or 'wheeling and dealing' and under its umbrella you'll find Negotiation.

# Which and when?

But which of the Five Basics do you use, and when? In order to make this decision you'll have to come up with the answers to a number of questions: 'How much time do we have – or are willing to use?', 'How important is it that we resolve this conflict?', 'Which of these styles have we used before?', 'What was our experience with them?' All of these, and others, are questions that must be asked, and answered. You may, for example, have limited time available or you may feel that the conflict is unimportant and not be bothered whether it is resolved or not. You may also have been 'ripped-off' in a previous win–lose situation and may, for good reason, not wish to repeat the experience. But you may also have experienced the value and benefits of either a collaborative or compromise situation and may wish to make sure that this happens again.

All of these and other factors mean that choosing the 'right' style of conflict management isn't easy. The stakes may be high, your prestige or reputation may be 'on the line', or you may be in a situation in which the money involved may be such that you can ill afford to lose.

But help is at hand. For when you fit these five styles into what is known as the classic Win–Lose matrix, then we find that this decision becomes a lot easier. For when you look at this (see Figure 1.1) what you'll see is that Negotiation, which is a particular and special form of the Compromise style of conflict management, allows you to break out of the traditional Win–Lose way of looking at things.

Negotiation adds another dimension; it is about results, outcomes, and upshots, rather than who wins or who loses. It takes you away from the process-led or 'this-is-the-way-we-do-things' myopia of the Collaboration, Avoidance, Competition and Accommodation styles of conflict management.

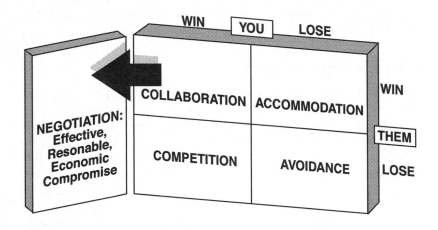

**Figure 1.1  Winning and losing – the options**

Negotiation creates outcomes that are acceptable to everyone involved and does so in ways that are economic. There are no extended tortuous dialogues in Negotiation; its pathway leads you directly to the endpoint you desire, and it achieves that without excessive use of time or money. What all of this tells you is that if you want an economic, effective and realistic way of resolving conflict, then Negotiation is the answer.

But before you go on explore the detail of the 'how' and 'why' of negotiating, you must find out about its 'what' and 'when'.

# What and when?

One of the best ways of starting to find out about the 'what' of something is to take a look at the ways in which other people have described or defined it. A good place to do that is in a dictionary and the *Oxford English Dictionary* tells us that when you or I negotiate we 'hold communication or conference (with another) for the purpose of arranging some matter by mutual agreement'. It also tells us that when we negotiate we 'discuss a matter with a view to some settlement or compromise'. Other dictionaries write of 'the transaction of business', 'settling issues by discussion and bargaining, attempting to come to terms' and 'conferring and seeking agreement'. Negotiation is often seen as having much in common with the acts of Bargaining and Bartering. The verbs that cluster around these include: trafficking, trading, buying, selling, haggling and wrangling. Bargaining, the dictionary tells us, involves the exchange of money and goods and often implies an 'antagonism of interest' – while bartering means the exchange of goods for goods. But both of these lack the broad sweep of Negotiation. Indeed, if you think about it you will soon arrive at a point at which you can see that both Bargaining and Bartering are actually limited forms of Negotiation. If you follow this trail to its end, you will soon begin to realize the considerable variety of the negotiation. A negotiation can, for example, take place between groups – such as trade unions, companies, corporations or governments – or between individuals – such as buyers and sellers. It can be formal in nature – involving what can be seen as rituals and ceremonies – or informal and seamlessly integrated into our day-by-day commonplace exchanges. The outcomes of a negotiation, which can be seen as an agreement, can be just as various. These can, for example, be about how much people will be paid and for what, how people will behave under certain circumstances or what will be paid for certain goods or services. These outcomes can also include a 'story' – negotiated and agreed by those involved – which describes to the outside world the 'what' and 'why' of the negotiations. This sort of outcome is often seen on our television news programmes.

Literature and films give us images of negotiations conducted in smoke-filled rooms by two dedicated individuals. Poker-faced and shirt sleeved, they slog out an agreement which is then carried out to the waiting crowds. Such images tell us much about the complexity and variety of Negotiation. But when you distil this all down, what you come to are the Six Core Characteristics of Negotiation.

## The core characteristics

All negotiations, whatever they are about and wherever they take place, have Six Core Characteristics. These tell us that all negotiations:

- ■ involve people – acting either as individuals, representatives, singly or in groups
- ■ have the thread of conflict running through them – from beginning to end
- ■ use well-established ways of exchanging things – such as bargaining or bartering
- ■ are almost always face-to-face – drawing strongly on the use of the spoken word, gesture and facial expression
- ■ are all about the future
- ■ reach a conclusion by a decision that is taken jointly.

## The definition

You have now arrived at the point where we can put the essential nature of a negotiation into words. This is usually called a definition, and our definition tells us that:

NEGOTIATION is the way that
people identify mutually acceptable
decisions and agree the what and
how of future actions

This tells us about the core people aspect of negotiation, reminds us that any decisions taken must be jointly taken and underlines the futurity of what we agree.

# What next?

Now you can begin to move on to look at the how and why of negotiation – such as where and when it takes place and the ways in which skilled negotiators behave. You'll do that in the three following sections of this book; sections that tell you how you can:

Prepare for your negotiations

Carry out your negotiations, and

Complete your negotiations.

In each of these you'll be looking at the key points and skills that you need to enhance and extend your negotiating skills.

# Checklist ✔

In this chapter you have seen that:

negotiating is something that we all do, all of the time. ☐

negotiations take place about almost everything in our lives. ☐

negotiation is the most effective way of resolving conflict. ☐

all negotiations have six core characteristics:

1 they involve people – acting either as individuals, representatives, singly or in groups ☐

2 have the thread of conflict running through them ☐

3 use bargaining or bartering so you can exchange things ☐

4 almost always involve face-to-face contact ☐

5 are about the future ☐

6 arrive at a jointly taken decision. ☐

■ negotiation can be defined as the way that people identify mutually acceptable decisions and agree the what and how of future actions.          ☐

## Part One
# PREPARING FOR YOUR NEGOTIATION

*You can't hatch chickens from fried eggs.*

Pennsylvania Dutch Proverb

# 2 | SETTING OBJECTIVES

*What is the use of running when we are not on the right road?*

**German Proverb**

Before you go any further, we need to take a look at Preparation. Preparation is an under-rated art. It is not just important to your negotiation, it is *vital*. It is the first of those key steps that take you along the road to success in those negotiations. Like the Scouts say: 'Be prepared'. Good preparation builds a solid foundation for your negotiation. It gives you the confidence that you need to be successful. The other option – bad, limited or even no preparation – is a poor alternative. It will leave you exposed, put you on thin ice. If you're like most people, you'll cut corners on your preparation. You'll do this because you're busy, haven't got time, can't be bothered. But if you're going to be a good negotiator then you need to make the time, to change your priorities, to get bothered. But this, your preparation, shouldn't be indiscriminate or unfocused. To contribute to success in your negotiations your preparation should be aimed at achieving an over-arching objective – that of making sure that you go into your negotiation knowing more than the person you face. If you don't make the grade on this, then you're at risk. If you do make it, then you have the upper hand – even if you're facing the greatest negotiator in the world. When you prepare well, when you make the grade in your preparation, you begin a journey – one that has you stepping up to success through a chain of linked actions.

# Getting started

The first step that you take in your preparations is a simple and straightforward one – it is that of deciding what it is that you want to achieve. Seems obvious, doesn't it? But you'd be surprised how many people don't do it or if they try to, don't do it in enough detail. It is not enough to say 'I want to be paid more' or 'I want to get a good price for my old car.' You have to be specific, clear cut, precise. You need to ask and answer questions like 'How much more?' or 'What's a good price?' and these answers, as you'll see later, have to be realistic.

---

**CAR FOR SALE (PART I)**

Peter wanted to sell his car. It was getting old, 90,000 miles on the clock.

'I wonder how much I'll be able to get for it' he said to his friend, Chris. 'How much do you want?' was Chris's answer. '$1,000 – enough to put down the deposit on a new motor bike' Peter replied. Chris smiled – he'd ridden in Peter's car, felt the bumps in the road through its worn suspension, struggled with the discomfort of the sagging passenger seat. He could see that this was going to be another of those long discussions.

---

But deciding what you think you want is just the first step. For if your negotiations are going to be successful you'll have to go further than this. You have to be able to:

- discriminate between what you *want* and what you *need*,
- identify your limits, and
- prepare yourself to reach an endpoint that, as you saw in Chapter 1, needs to be acceptable to everyone involved.

Let's take a look at each of these in turn.

# Needs and wants

Needing something and wanting it are subtly, but significantly, different. Let's say, for example, that you're looking at replacing the family car. The station wagon you bought second-hand some five years ago has had its day. Two kids and a dog, camping holidays and the weekly expedition to the supermarket have all left their mark – in some cases, literally and indelibly. What are you going to replace it with – another station wagon or estate car, one of those new MPVs? Maybe – since money's a little easier this year – you could get one of those huge, new, swish Swedish executive saloons. All of these are possible. But, the answer, I'm afraid, is inevitable. For, while you may *want* a swish new Swedish executive saloon, the pressures of limited resources and the demands of a growing family mean that what you really *need* is a vehicle that can, economically and reliably, transport your family around. And that's another station wagon or estate car. Similarly, in your workplace, you may *want* a new go-faster computer with super graphics and one of those new TFT flat screens, but what you really *need* is an office chair that's half-way decent to sit in for more than half an hour.

Drawing this line, seeing the differences between your wants and your needs, is an important step. Get it right and you start off on the right foot. Get it wrong and you put at risk the rest of your negotiations – you may even find yourself unable to implement their outcomes successfully.

# First, second and third

Identifying your needs starts you off. But it isn't all that you need to do. For what you now need to do is to colour in the outline that your need identification has given you. In the example above – the one about replacing the family station wagon or estate car – you saw how it was that your needs rather than your wants led you to the conclusion that you needed another station wagon. What you need to do now is to add detail to this need. Features like seating capacity, reliability, access to servicing, fuel economy, trade-in deals and price are now the issues. What you have to do now is really quite simple – you have to prioritize these features – to decide the order that you rate them in. For example, you might feel that seating capacity is the most important feature, followed by boot (or trunk) capacity, and then reliability. If you were doing a list – and that's not a bad idea – you'd do it this way:

---

## KEY FEATURES

1    Seating capacity

2    Boot size

3    Reliability

---

Note that we're talking about functionality here – rather than appearance or fashion. But the next door family – the Jones's (no kids, no dog and both at work) – may rate factors such as styling and speed as more important. Their list would probably look like this:

---

## KEY FEATURES

1    Speed

2    Looks

3    Colour

---

Deciding your priorities is important – it gives your negotiating an edge, it sharpens your focus. You can be sure that the person you're negotiating with will have done it, and their list will be different to yours. The car dealer that you face in your negotiations will have a list that's quite different from yours and may look something like this:

## KEY FEATURES

1    Selling more cars

2    Getting highest possible price

3    Getting or keeping you as a customer

We'll take a longer and more detailed look at the ways and means that you can use to find out more about the person you're negotiating with, and what makes them tick, in the next chapter. For now, you need to remember that the over-arching objective of your preparation is to make sure that you go into your negotiation knowing more than they do. These initial steps – of identifying what answers your need and then prioritizing its features – have taken you partway down that road. What you need to do now is to paint in the background and choose the frame for the picture of your need that you've just coloured in. The materials that you use to do this are *facts*.

# Finding the facts

Facts are fascinating things – they can entertain you, amaze you, thrill you and scare you. But in your negotiations they give you power and authority. They give you, for example, the confidence to walk away from or challenge the salesperson who tells you that Sony doesn't make the small TV with a built-in video recorder that you saw in the catalogue or on the Sony web site and that your son's set his heart on.

Let's take a look at where you can find your facts.

## Consumer reports

Most countries have consumer organizations: in the UK it is the Consumers Association; in the States it is Consumer Reports. These and other organizations are dedicated to testing, rating, comparing and analysing the performance of a wide range of consumer goods from microwaves to mortgages and paints to potties. But their views aren't just based on laboratory tests, useful as these are. They often poll their members on their experience of reliability and fault levels. Past test reports are usually available – often by fax. Use them!

## Libraries

In my view there's nothing quite so wonderful as a well-stocked, well-run, library. They are without doubt *the* most effective source of information you can find. They exist all over the place – try your local authority or town council, the nearby high school or the out-of-town university. Wherever you find them, they'll contain a whole host of information sources. Reports, surveys, lists, test data – it's all there; all you have to do is go and get it. Doing that, of course, means getting to the library and then finding your way around it. There are usually library people who'll help you to do the latter – the former is up to you.

## The Internet

Much has been written about the Internet and many of you will have experienced the joys and frustrations of being on-line. For those of you who haven't, the Internet is, put simply, a collection of computers that spans the world. All of these are linked together by some hi-tech communications systems. But don't get worried – all you need to know is how to link into that communications net using a computer, a modem and a telephone line. With these and the help of an Internet service provider (ISP) you'll be able to access computers all over the world. Why should you want to do that? Well, doing that can put you in touch with an amazing amount of information and an incredible number of services. You can access weather satellites, order your groceries, visit university libraries, buy a car, send e-mail, or find out where your long-lost friend lives now. To do this you need some software called a web browser. Your ISP will provide this – the current favourites are Netscape Navigator or Microsoft's Internet Explorer. With this you can jazz about the Internet to your heart's content. But searching for information – as you'll do in preparation for your negotiations – requires you to be more focused than that. To get this focus you'll use web sites that provide you with a search facility – you tell them what you want to know and they tell you what web sites to visit to find it. Web addresses for a couple of these and some other interesting sites are listed in the Further Reading section at the back of this book. The main advantage that the Internet has is its immediacy – you do it when you want to rather than in someone else's opening hours – and the fact that you access the Internet from your home, office or wherever your computer is. Its disadvantages include the fact that access can be slow and sometimes expensive – depending upon the local call rates that give you telephone access to your ISP and the deal that you have with that ISP.

## Walking, shopping and looking

It doesn't matter how much you search or how many surveys or test reports that you read, you still can't beat the unique information that you get by walking and talking, touching and feeling, or even smelling and tasting. If you're buying a house, you'll have used your local library or the Internet to check up on the history, geography, weather and even the bus or train timetables of the area around your new potential home. You'll have talked to the town council about their plans for the area and researched the competition between possible sources for your finance. Now you need to walk the ground, talk to the neighbours, ask around in the bars and pubs.

Let's say you want to buy a new refrigerator. Consumer reports and tests will have told you what's available and what's reliable or not reliable. Now you need to get out and look at them, open the doors, remove the trays and look at the instruction books. While you're doing this you'll probably begin to get some idea about whether the salesperson knows what she or he's talking about and, most important, whether a deal is possible. Take notes – you'll be surprised how easily you forget or how one salesperson will tell you a different tale when you go back. All of this you get by walking, looking and shopping – but not buying.

## Other bits and bobs

The world today is full of magazines and newspaper articles about what we should or shouldn't do in almost every part of our lives. Some of these are good but a lot of them aren't. But most of them contain nuggets of information that we can use to our advantage. Good examples of this sort of information include the 'best six' of saving account or mortgage rates that you get in your Saturday or Sunday newspaper supplements, or the used car price handbooks that you can buy off the magazine rack in your supermarket. Others include the price of gold or the £/$ or $/Yen exchange rates. Collect them and/or note down when and where they appear – you never know when they'll come in useful.

## Review

Let's just check where you've got to.

You started by  ■ **Identifying** what your need – rather than your want – is

Then you  ■ **Prioritized** the important features of that need

And then you  ■ **Researched** the ways in which that need with those prioritized features might be answered.

Here are a couple of examples of what these three steps can generate:

| | | |
|---|---|---|
| **NEED** | Station wagon/ Estate car | Combination fridge-freezer |
| **PRIORITY FEATURES** | 1. Seating for 6<br>2. Boot large enough for large dog<br>3. Reliable | 1. Large freezer<br>2. Large fridge bottle rack<br>3. Adjustable shelves |
| **RESEARCH OUTCOMES** | Info. on priority and other features and how they vary between makes and models. | Info. on priority and other features and how they vary between makes and models. |

Price info.                    Price info.
Dealer info.                   Dealer info.
Second hand value info.

Now you've got to the point where you must take some decisions about the *value* that you put on the car, fridge, house etc. that you're going to negotiate about.

## Best, worst and expected

Value is a funny old thing. It all depends on what something is (or appears to be), how many people want it, and how much they or you are prepared to pay or exchange for it. We can see this on the commodity markets of the world when poor harvests cause the price of soya or olive oil to leap skywards. Even the value of money itself fluctuates – moving up and down with the tides of the world money markets. Most times, the values that things have are relative: to other commodities, goods and services, to the value of money itself and to the need that people have for them.

But the value that *you* put on something is a personal thing. That value, like beauty, is in the eye of the beholder. This means that some of us will place high values on goods, services or commodities that others would not consider buying, and low values on other commodities, goods and services that others rate highly. Recognizing this is important, for the value that you give to something plays an important role in your negotiations over it.

One of the best ways of doing this is to try to put numbers to what you'd settle for in the forthcoming negotiation. For example, if you're buying something, there'll be:

- a price you'd be very happy to settle at
- a price above which you'll not go, and
- a price that your experience and research tells you that you'll probably finish up paying.

If you're selling something there'll be:

- a price you'd be very happy to settle at
- a price below which you will not go, and
- a price that your experience and research tells you that you'll probably finish up selling for.

These values – for buyer and seller – can be described as:
- the ideal value
- the maximum or minimum value, and
- the realistic value.

When we bring them together, as in Figure 2.1, we begin to see their relative positions. Later, in Part Two, we'll see how you and the person you're negotiating with can move from your positions at the outer limits of this value range into what is called the Bargaining Zone (see Chapter 9). It is in this zone that you and they will find the agreement that you both desire.

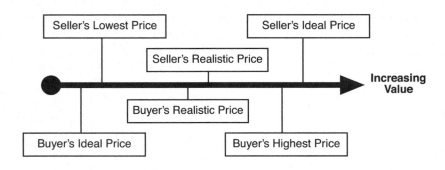

**Figure 2.1  Selling and buying**

For now, what you must do is to decide what are the values, prices or costs that you think are right for your negotiation. Think hard about them – don't jump at the first figure that comes into your head – and be prepared to stick by them during your negotiations. Remember that the person you're going to negotiate with will also have worked out his or her set of values and will be just as prepared to stick by them as you are yours.

---

### CAR FOR SALE (PART II)

Chris sighed – at last they'd got there! 'Let's check it out,' he said to Peter.

'You'd be delighted if you got $1,000 for your car but you must have a minimum of $500 and you think that from all the stuff in the Green Book you're likely to get about $625 to $650.'

'That's it,' said Peter. 'Great' said Chris '– now can I go home?'

---

# What next?

Now you can move on to the next phase of your preparation – that of finding out about the other person – the Other Side.

# Checklist ✔

In this chapter you have seen that:

- ■ preparation is the key to the success of your negotiations. ☐
- ■ the first step that you take in your preparation is to decide what it is that you need rather than want. ☐
- ■ the second is to identify and prioritize the key features of what you need. ☐
- ■ the third step is to research, research and research. ☐
- ■ the final step of this stage of your preparation is to decide what are your ideal, minimum and realistic values. ☐

# 3 | THE OTHER SIDE

*It takes all sorts to make a world.*

**Proverb**

Now you've got the facts, now you know what it is that you need and now you know what it's most important features are. You've researched all the background stuff and, finally, you've decided what your ideal, minimum (or maximum) and realistic values are. So what comes next?

The answer is another of those simple and obvious ones – it's people. For people aren't just important to your negotiations – they're essential. Back at the beginning, in Chapter 1, you saw that all your negotiations involve people. These people negotiate for themselves, as you do when you purchase a new car, or they negotiate for a group of people, as when you negotiate on behalf of a group of neighbours with a common problem. They do it to answer their own needs (it's that car again!) or they do it to answer the needs of others – as you do when you negotiate on behalf of your employer or your family. These negotiations can be on a one-to-one basis or between groups or teams. Almost all of your negotiations will be face-to-face – they'll draw strongly on the rhythms and tides of your spoken words and be punctuated by your gestures and facial expressions (see Chapter 6). The ways in which you relate to or interact with all of these other people in your negotiations are complex, as are your motives for doing so. In this chapter you'll begin to look at the 'people' aspects of your negotiations – the Other Side. These are the people who have something that you want – or alternatively, who want something that you have. They are the other side of the negotiating table, the other side of the potential bargain and hopefully, by the time you've finished, the other side of your joint agreement. What you now need to do about these people might, at the first glance, seem impossible. For you need to get to know them, to find out what are their strengths and weaknesses, their idiosyncrasies and eccentricities, their blind spots and their areas of special expertise – and you need to do as much of that as you can *before* you meet them, *before* you sit across the negotiating table from them.

## Getting to know you

Whenever you negotiate with someone – whether you do or don't know them from before – there's always one thing that you can be sure about. You can be sure about this before you've met them, before you've even spoken to them and before you've done any of your research about them. And that, always sure-fire, thing is that they're human beings.

This will probably change at some point in the future. Some twenty-fifth-century Captain James T. Kirk will, no doubt, have to face the task of negotiating with an alien race. When that happens he'll probably find that their culture and values are very different from ours. But, until that happens, you can be pretty sure that the people that you face in your negotiations are what they appear to be – human beings. This is important. For it tells you – before you've even met them – that they have something in common with you. That is, that they have needs – as do you. But these needs, as you saw in Chapter 1, are never fully satisfied. You'll remember that Abraham Maslow told us that these needs sit in five groups, groups which are stacked on top of each other – as in a pyramid or a staircase – with the highest priority needs at the bottom. Food, warmth and shelter; protection and security; affection and attachment; reputation and recognition; self-fulfilment: that was their order on the 'staircase' and also the order in which they act on us. Except, of course, it is never that simple. Human beings are endlessly complex and to suggest that you, or I, behave in the ways that we do because of a single need or even a single group of needs is far from the truth. The needs and desires that we have as individuals and, indeed, the sort of people we are, result from the effects and results of a complex 'rag-bag' of heredity, our experiences, our body chemistry and our emotions. The ways in which we describe the behaviours that result from these needs and desires are often generalized and subjective. You might, for example, describe someone as being taciturn when they have little to say to you; you might also describe their behaviour as antisocial or say that they are close-mouthed. While some of these descriptions might be near to the truth, others might not be. In the variety and subjectivity of these descriptions there lies the risk that we might misunderstand or misinterpret their behaviour. If this happens while you are negotiating with them then it brings in its train the risk of failure. Nevertheless, despite all this complexity, it is possible to identify some patterns in this kaleidoscope of behaviour – patterns that will help you to understand the Other Side.

## Turning in or turning out

The terms *extroversion* and *introversion* were first used in the nineteenth century to describe the ways in which people behave. They soon became popular, appearing in several best-selling novels of the time. At that time, an extrovert was thought of as someone who was sociable, impulsive and carefree while an introvert was seen as unsociable, responsible and thoughtful. Since that time it has been realized that it is unrealistic to describe people as either just extrovert or introvert. The current view – backed by considerable research – is that it is possible to measure the degree of extroversion or introversion shown in a person's behaviour and to use this to locate that person on a scale with extroverts at one end, introverts at the other and ambiverts in the middle. The ways of behaving that change over this scale are sociability, impulsiveness, changeability, talkativeness, outgoingness, activity, liveliness, excitability and optimism – all of which are high for extroverts and low for introverts. Other studies suggest that most (about two-thirds) of our extroversion or introversion is inherited while the remaining one-third has environmental causes. In the extreme, extroverts:

     talk a lot – and loudly

     interrupt people and talk over the top of them

■ make introverts more introverted

     often make sure that they have to have the last word.

At the other extreme, introverts:

     are quiet and unresponsive

     often trigger extroverts into being more extroverted

     censor their ideas before they say them

     let other people do the talking.

It should be pretty obvious by now that a negotiation between an extreme extrovert and an extreme introvert is unlikely to generate the mutually acceptable agreements that we need to come out of our negotiations. But, fortunately, few of us lie at these extremes and most of us have learnt to modify our extroversion or introversion to suit the circumstances we find ourselves in. It is also worth remembering that the different roles needed in a team of negotiators– such as chairperson, ideas generator, finisher etc. – will require different levels of introversion and extroversion. But these aren't the only patterns that have been identified in the ways that we behave.

# Four points on the compass of behaviour

The early twentieth century was a time of enormous change in the way that people thought about and described human behaviour. During that time many new ideas – ideas that we now take for granted – were developed. Amongst these were the ideas of the Swiss psychologist, Carl Jung. While giving full justice to Jung's ideas is beyond the scope of this book, it is worth visiting some of them, albeit briefly, in order to help you to understand the different ways in which people, and particularly those on the other side of your negotiation, might behave.

Jung suggested that the ways in which we all interpret and react to the world around us can be described by using two 'dimensions' – dimensions with the opposing extremes of sensation and intuition and of thought and feeling – almost like the N–S and E–W dimensions on our compasses. According to him, we keep in touch with what is going on around us by using either our senses or our intuition. Similarly, we make decisions about that information by either thinking about it or, at the other extreme, having feelings about it. He then went on to use these two groups of opposites (sensation being opposite to intuition and thought being opposite to feeling) to describe four basic and different ways of behaving:

- **ST behaviour** that draws on sensation (S) and thought (T). This is present in people who make their way through life by using a combination of sensing and thinking. Their interpretations and judgements can be described as being based on logic and 'hard facts'.

- **IT behaviour** and the actions that go to make it up are seen to be shaped by intuition and ideas (I) and thought (T). In this sort of behaviour all the possible options are identified and worked through.

- **IF behaviour** uses a combination of intuition (I) and feelings (F). By and large, people who behave in this way are more concerned with values than they are with facts.

- **SF behaviour** has its roots in the senses (S) and feelings (F). People in this group make their judgements on a basis of what 'feels right' rather than what is logical or factual.

All of this gives us a framework within which we can place people's behaviour and from which we can try to anticipate and even influence the ways that they might behave. But take care – for, in reality, people are endlessly complex and when we put them in two-dimensional slots or boxes like those above they almost always behave in ways that surprise or even alarm us. What you need to do if you're going to avoid that mistake is to find out as much as you can about them.

## Playing the detective

Your need to 'play the detective' is not a playful or casual one. For if your negotiation is going to be successful, then you really do need to know everything that you can about everything to do with it. As we saw in the last chapter, you've already trawled your way through a large amount of information about whatever it is that answers your need. You'll have ferreted out the relevant consumer reports, scoured the dusty corners of your library and burnt up telephone time surfing the Internet. You'll have walked, shopped, looked and listened. You'll have walked the ground, talked to the neighbours, asked around in the bars and pubs, opened refrigerator doors, removed trays and drawers, and looked at the instruction books. While you've been doing all of this, you've probably begun to get some sense of the way the people that you're going to negotiate with do their business. Shopping-around trips like this can be seen as what the military might call 'low profile reconnaissance missions'. We can use them to find out whether the salespeople in Shop A know what they're talking about or whether the salespeople in Shop B are open to deals. This is the sort of information that we need to know about the Other Side. It tells us about their strengths and weaknesses, gives us points about their 'know-how' and their 'don't know-how'. But this is just the beginning of what you must find out.

## Past and future

Some of the information that you must now find out about these people will be hard-fact and certain in nature – telling us, for example, what percentage of their negotiations had been successful or what discounts they gave last year. But some of it will be far less certain. This will be the sort of information that is based on opinions or views. But despite this, it is useful information. It will tell you things like what other people's opinions of the Other Side are, or what is rumoured about their financial position. But whatever the source, nature or certainty of this information, it will tell you:

■ what the other side has done in the past, and

■ what they might do in their negotiations with you, i.e. in the future.

The connection between these is both strong and obvious. For if you can see what they've done in their past negotiations, then you can use this information to guess what they might do in your negotiation. These guesses about their future actions will also reach out to touch the present – a present that contains the decisions that you will soon make about the ways and means of your future negotiation.

# History

Henry Ford claimed that history – or at least what he thought was history – was 'more or less bunk'. But is this true, or can the past provide us with the foundations of our future successes? The answer lies, as is so with most things, in the way that you look at them. For example, when you face a negotiator who has a track record of being a successful negotiator, then you can either take this to mean that:

■ you'll have little chance of 'winning', or
■ that he or she conducts her negotiations in an effective and professional manner.

In reality, having a track record like that means that the latter of these conclusions is probably nearer the truth. You can then heave a sigh of relief, for dealing with someone who negotiates in that way is a lot easier than dealing with an amateur. Similarly, you can either view the past as a heavy load of obligations and must-dos that will lead you to an obvious endpoint, or you can view that same past as a series of completed lessons – something that provides a data base for you to use when you decide how you're going to do it now. Successful negotiators do the latter. They use the past to map out the 'how' and 'when' of the other side's likely behaviour, they use it to analyse the ways that previous negotiations were carried out.

If you are going to do this, then there's some questions that you need to ask – questions that should be targeted at getting the information that you need so that you can be sure that you know everything that you need to know about the other side. These questions should, for example, start off with the obvious ones such as:

■ who are the other side?
■ what are their names and positions?
■ have you met them before?
■ if yes, under what circumstances?

Once you've got this basic information, the next set of questions follows on logically:

are they experienced negotiators?

if not, how inexperienced are they?

what can you find out about how they behaved in their previous negotiations?

are any of them new in their jobs, and hence needing to prove something?

The third group of questions probes further:

if you are negotiating with a team or group of people, has there been any sign of conflict or differences of opinion amongst them in the past?

what can you find out about the range and spread of the best, worst and expected values that they used in other negotiations?

were there signs that they'd done all of the research needed in these past negotiations?

if they did, were there any patterns in the outcomes that they set out to achieve?

■ is there any evidence that some features of these outcomes were more important to them than others?

These are just the basic questions about the past of the Other Side. When you start probing you'll find that other questions – more specific or more relevant to your negotiation – will crop up. Go for as much information as you can. Leave no stone unturned and remember – if you don't ask, then you'll never get an answer.

## Futures

If you get answers to the above questions then you'll have a good sense of the what, how and why of the other side's previous negotiations. What you need to do now is to use this and other information that you might find to make educated guesses as to what they might do in your negotiation. Some of these guesses about their future actions will be hedged about with uncertainty; some of them will be conditional upon the other side repeating their past patterns of negotiating behaviour. But despite this uncertainty, these guesses are important, as you'll see in the next chapter when you read about the decisions that you will soon make about the ways and means of your future negotiation. But, until then, let's see what we can find out about the future actions of the other side. For example:

- do they have enough authority to make whatever you agree with them stick – or do they have to get it all confirmed by someone else?
- will they have done their research – identified their wants and needs?
- if so, can you find out what they are and whether any of them are more important or powerful than the others?
- what can you find out about the range and spread of the best, worst and expected values that they'll use in your negotiation?
- what sort of pressure are they under – do they have to complete in the near future or to a given price?

Getting answers to all of these is important even if they are guesses which are hedged around with uncertainty.

## Hidden agendas

Even when you've answered all of these and other questions, and assessed what you've found out, everything may not be as it seems. For there still may be a hidden factor, one that exerts a strong influence over your negotiation. For example, you may find that, surprisingly and suddenly, you are able to negotiate a good sale to a company. You've been knocking, unsuccessfully, on their door for some months and then, suddenly – you're in. You're selling and they're buying. Just after you close the sale, their buyer says something that makes you realize what's been going on. You realize that you've been given the order to teach his usual supplier a lesson! This sort of thing is called a 'hidden agenda'.

Hidden agendas are very common. They can be just as important as their more visible cousins and they are often more persistent or long-lived. We all have them. We send our kids to the movies not because the film they're going to see is good entertainment or educational, but because we want some time alone with our partners; we help other people because we want to be liked; and we volunteer for tough projects at work because we want to get promotion. Having hidden agendas isn't the problem – but spotting them is! Because of this you need to be mindful of and cautious about hidden agendas in your negotiations. They can be as damaging as the hidden reefs that rip the bottom out of a boat. But watching for them isn't enough. You also need to find out – as a part of your preparation – as much as you can about the other side's motives. When you know what 'turns them on', then you not only know how to avoid their hidden agendas, you may also find new and unexpected ways of reaching agreement with them.

## What next?

In the next chapter you'll find one of the key phases of your preparation for negotiation – that of finding out what are your strategic and tactical options.

## Checklist ✔

In this chapter you were reminded that:

■ people are key to your negotiations.  ☐

and you saw that:

■ you need to get to know as much as you can about the people on the other side of your negotiations.  ☐

■ the other side also has needs.  ☐

■ the ways that people behave can be partially described by degrees of introversion or extroversion.  ☐

■ another framework for describing the way people behave uses the way that they use their senses, intuition, thinking and feelings.  ☐

■ you need to find out as much as you can about:
  – how the other side did it before – their negotiating history.  ☐
  – how they might do it in your future negotiations.  ☐
  – their motives and hidden agendas.  ☐

# 4 STRATEGIES AND TACTICS

*In baiting a mouse-trap with cheese, always leave room for the mouse.*

**Saki**

If you ask a military person what the words strategy and tactic mean, he (or she) will probably come up with a definition something like this one out of a military dictionary:

'Strategy differs materially from tactic; the latter belonging only to the mechanical movement of bodies set in motion by the former.'

If, on the other hand, you asked a business school professor or a business analyst what they meant by a firm's strategy they'd probably come up with something like this:

'Strategy is the theme that unifies a firm's business.'

But when you use these words – strategy and tactics – in your negotiation you'll find that they take on meanings that are subtly, but significantly, different. For the strategy that you adopt in your negotiation gives it an overarching policy or line of action. It will link together or unify all that you do in that negotiation. Its objective is the attainment of a number of defined outcomes. But, while this strategy provides you with an outcome or endpoint, it is your tactics that will tell you how to get there. These tactics are about things like the detail of your actions and the nature of your responses to the other side's ploys.

Let's look at a simple, almost everyday example. Let's say that you want to travel from London to Paris. Put simply, the strategy for your journey would be to travel pleasantly and economically and to arrive in Paris on 3 July at 8.30 am local time. Your tactics would be about the how and when of that journey. You could travel by plane, train, boat or car – either singly or in combination – and you could do so at night or during the day. The decisions that you take about these are your tactical decisions. In practice, the line between strategy and tactics is never as clear-cut as we might intend; reality, expediency and the interrelationship between these two often blurs the divide. There is also, whatever we might intend, the difference between what you plan for your strategy and your tactics, and what you are able to achieve. Nevertheless, deciding what strategy you will follow in your negotiation and what tactics you will follow to achieve that are an important part of the preparations that you make for your negotiation.

# Winning or losing

When you read about negotiations in the newspapers or hear about them on TV or radio programmes, they are often described as having 'winners' or 'losers'. In high profile industrial disputes or in compensation cases, it is a victory for one side and a defeat for the other. But negotiating is something that you do *with* someone – not *to* them. This means that, in reality, these sorts of negotiation generally consist of discussions between professional negotiators – discussions that are aimed at reaching agreements, agreements to which everybody involved is a party, agreements that contain benefits to both sides.

Taking this step – turning away from the adversarial combat of the win–lose approach and stepping towards the creation of jointly agreed deals and trade-offs – is the first of your strategic decisions. It is not an optional one. For if you're going to be an effective negotiator, the acts of generating jointly agreed outcomes and working together for the long run are *musts* rather than options. But, having said that, you do stand a good chance of meeting others who don't see things that way, who aren't effective negotiators. Their interests will be in the short term; they will be after the 'quick buck'. Negotiators like this can take advantage of the ill prepared or unwary. As an effective negotiator you must be able to cope with this aggressive 'win–lose' style, and later in this chapter we look at the tactics that enable you to do that. In the meantime, let's look at the options that you face when choosing the strategy you'll follow in your negotiation – a negotiation that you'll do *with* rather than *to* the people on the other side of the negotiating table.

# Strategic options

When you look back at what you've already decided you might think that you've already chosen your negotiating strategy. You've decided what you need, identified its most important features and researched all that you can about it. You've even decided what, for you, are its ideal, minimum and realistic values. So what's left to do?

Let's try and answer that question by being particular. Let's assume, for example that you (and your partner) have decided that you need a new freezer or cold box. After some discussion you decide that, for you, the most important features of the freezer are:

---

### KEY FEATURES

1    A small footprint – so that it can fit in the corner of your Kitchen

2    A large enough capacity

3    Be easy to access

---

These priorities lead you to conclude that you need an upright freezer with pull-out drawers. You read the consumer reports and tests and go out into the stores to look at them, you open the doors, remove the trays and look at the instruction books. You talk to the salespeople in the stores, find out whether they know what they're talking about, test whether a deal is possible. Finally, after balancing your budget and talking to the loan manager at the bank, you arrive at the point where you can define the desired outcome of

your negotiation. That is that you know the make, model and price
of the freezer that you want. So what's next?

What's next is that you need to decide how you're going to get that
freezer into your kitchen or garage at a price you can live with.
Your route to this lies through the store and, more specifically,
through a salesperson. Because you've read the previous chapter of
this book, you'll have done your homework. You'll have a name –
you noted it down when you did your research visit – and you've
timed your negotiating visit for when the store isn't busy. You've
also found out as much as you can about their sales incentive plan
from the recruitment section of the store's Internet site and a
neighbour who used to work there. You may even have been able to
find out something about the salesperson's interests and
background. If all this seems a lot of work just to buy a freezer,
remember that the same needs and principles will apply when the
stakes are much higher – when you buy your next house, for
example, or when you're negotiating at work over that new
mainframe computer. If you get it right with the small buys – when
the risk is lower and you can more easily afford to make mistakes –
then you'll get it right on the big ones. So are you ready now – can
you begin?

Not yet – because before you get into the fine grain, the nitty-gritty
of your negotiation, you still have at least three decisions to make.
These are about:

- whether you go it alone or as part of a team of
  negotiators
- the order and content of your 'things to do' list for
  your negotiations, and, finally
- what tactics you'll use.

Let's look at them in that order.

## Teams and roles

In many of the formal negotiations of our workplace, the working
units are teams. In management–union negotiations the union team
will, typically, consist of a full-time union official who is supported
by a group of local or plant union people. The management team
will be headed by the plant manager, backed up by the personnel

and production managers. Similarly, in a negotiation over the sale of a large (and very expensive) mainframe computer, the computer people will probably field a mixed team, consisting of salespeople and technical people. The benefits of having a team are considerable: you have a wider spread of knowledge and ability, and team members can take on different tasks and even different roles. You can have a chairperson or leader who manages what's happening, a 'bad guy' who always takes a critical hard line about everything that the other side says or does, and a 'good guy' who pushes for agreement and sees the other side's point of view. In large teams these roles can get quite complex (for more information see Further Reading section, page 174). What is needed if the negotiating team is going to work is a team that:

- is large enough – but not too large
- has a balanced mix of skills, abilities and experience
- has worked out the detail of who does what and when
- consists of members who trust each other.

But not all of our negotiations are as significant or as formal as this. Many of them are informal and concerned with resolving the differences and conflicts that crop up in our work-a-day worlds. In these, and in the negotiations that we carry out in the markets and malls, the use of specially created teams is obviously inappropriate and unnecessary. But having said that, let's not forget that we are often members of other teams, teams that exist for other purposes than negotiating – such as the teams that we form with our families and our partners. So when you go to negotiate over your freezer it makes sense to do that with your partner or a friend. Doing this isn't an admission of weakness or inability. On the contrary, it is actually a sensible and rational choice that recognizes the fact that two negotiators, working together and doing so in previously agreed ways, can synergize into a whole that is greater than the sum of their parts. With this sort of team on your side, success is certainly a step or more nearer.

## Agendas

The word agenda, so the *Oxford English Dictionary* tells us, means 'a list of things to be done'. We've already seen the power of the hidden agenda that the other side of your negotiation might have. The agenda that you set for your negotiation is just as powerful. For when you create an agenda for your negotiation you define its content; you set up the boundary posts of the negotiating area. Creating a written agenda is a very powerful, often challenging, act and in many formal negotiations this agenda itself can be the subject of protracted negotiations. The risk of this happening can be reduced by creating and circulating a draft agenda which can be converted into an agreed formal version after informal feedback discussions. Doing it this way not only shares the task – you're literally doing it with them – it also:

■ reduces the chance of surprise items that might otherwise 'pop-up' in the course of negotiations, and

■ gives you some insight into the other side's 'wish list'.

But most informal negotiations don't have agendas – unless you create them. Doing so is easier than you'd think. It's an easy but clear 'I'd like to talk about . . .' sort of statement that, of course, is best made at the beginning. Putting this in writing is unnecessary – except in your personal notes.

---

### VERBAL AGENDAS

It was time for the usual annual wage negotiations. Fred, the personnel manager, had done his homework. He'd found out that the union was also going to bring up the issue of medical insurance. So when the meeting started, in his office, he got in first. 'We're meeting', he said, 'to discuss your claim for an increase in wage rates, but before we start I thought it would be useful if I went over the factual background so that we've all got the same picture.' He knew that using the phrase 'before we start' would probably silence any objections to him speaking first – and it did. He went on to review the history of recent negotiations over payment systems, dropping as he did a hint that fringe benefits like medical insurance would become taxable as a 'payment-in-kind' at the next government tax review. In the subsequent discussions, the union kept their proposal to wage rates.

## Tactics

If strategy is the long view of a negotiation, then tactics are its here-and-now. They are about the nitty-gritty of negotiation; they are about the actions that we take and the reactions that we have. For that reason, many of them are negotiation-specific. That is to say that they relate to the circumstances and rhythms of a particular negotiation – rather than to all negotiations. But, whatever their content might be and whenever they are used, these tactics all have one characteristic: that to be effective they must be complementary to, and/or compatible with, your chosen strategy. If they fall at this hurdle then your use of them runs the risk of being disruptive, of interrupting, breaking up the rhythms of your negotiating. So count to ten before you react to the other side's actions and take care that the actions you take are thoughtful and compatible with your overall strategy.

Here are some examples:

| TACTIC | COMMENTS |
| --- | --- |
| If you're selling, start high then trade down, and if you're buying start low then trade up. | *It is almost impossible to trade up or down later* |
| Don't exaggerate | *Exaggerated facts can prove embarrassing – later* |
| When you've got an agreement – leave | *Hanging about can lead to second thoughts* |
| Respect the other side's conventions | *When in Rome do as the Romans do* |
| Keep your word | *Not doing what you'd said you'd do leads to doubt and doubt leads to mistrust and mistrust **doesn't** lead to agreement.* |
| Take a pause | *Pauses are powerful. They can:*<br>■ *help you keep your cool*<br>■ *make you appear thoughtful*<br>■ *slow things down* |

| TACTIC (continued) | COMMENTS (continued) |
|---|---|
| Get their shopping list before you start bargaining | *It is easier to sell when you know what they want to buy* |
| Never give a concession – always trade it | *What's not paid for in some way is never valued* |
| Leave the other side feeling that they've got as good a deal as you have | *Next time you'll both get an even better deal* |
| Deadlines are always negotiable | *Time can be elastic* |
| Stress the advantages of your offer | *Advantages are always better than costs* |
| Use emotion consciously but honestly | *Instant emotional reactions can sink your strategy and most of us can smell a false one a mile away* |
| Make use of silence | *Silence can be thoughtful or a considered response to aggression or an unacceptable offer* |
| Be realistic | *Don't expect perfection* |
| Don't push too hard | *This can lead to deadlock and stalemate* |

# Aggressive negotiators

Earlier in this chapter we noted that, with the world being what it is, you stand a good chance of meeting negotiators who are aggressive. These will be the negotiators who believe in the 'I win – you lose' style of negotiating. They will be after the 'quick kill' and an instant return rather than building for the future. Negotiators like this can catch you unawares and will certainly take advantage of the ill-prepared negotiator. If you're going to be an effective negotiator, then you must be able to cope with this aggression. Here are some examples of the ways in which you can do that:

| THEIR TACTIC | YOUR RESPONSE |
|---|---|
| Threats | *Refuse to negotiate under pressure. Tell them you'll only make concessions if and when they come up with a reasoned argument based on facts. Be prepared to withdraw.* |
| Insults | *Keep cool, don't lose your temper, get angry or trade insults. Restate your position, coolly and clearly. Warn them that continued insults can only result in negotiations being broken off.* |
| Intimidation | *This is sometimes subtle and not easy to detect. If you spot it, remember it's just a ploy. Don't allow yourself to be pressured into an early agreement or to give away concessions.* |
| Divide and conquer | *Another ploy, which you can counter by good preparation or by taking a break and resolving the differences in your team.* |
| Bluff and bluster | *Call their bluff, refuse to be forced into an agreement on this basis. Question all their statements and demand to see evidence if you think their claims are spurious.* |

Remember that, even in the face of this aggression, you still have the upper hand. After all, if you've done your preparation well, you're not only better prepared than they are – you're also better informed. Their aggression will only work if you allow it to.

### WHAT SHOULD SHE DO?

Joanne could feel the tension rising. She and her boss had been talking about next year's budget for her department for a while and he was beginning to get aggressive. The number and frequency of his interruptions was creeping up and she could see that he wasn't happy. He was sitting there, glaring at her, not responding to anything she said. 'I'll start to get angry', she told herself, 'if this goes on for much longer.'
What should she do?

# What next?

The next chapter continues with your preparation and takes a look at how you can influence the 'where', 'when' and 'how' of your negotiations.

# Checklist ✔

In this chapter you have seen:

the strategy you adopt for your negotiations should be designed to link together or unify all that you do in that negotiation. ☐

the tactics that you use will be concerned with things like the detail of your actions and responses to the other side's ploys. ☐

negotiating is something that you do *with* someone – not *to* them. ☐

you'll need to decide:

– whether you go it alone or as part of a team of negotiators ☐
– the order and content of your 'things to do' list for your negotiations ☐
– what tactics you'll use. ☐

negotiating teams need to be carefully chosen and well prepared. ☐

different negotiations need different tactics. ☐

an aggressive negotiator will only gain the upper hand if you allow him or her to. ☐

# 5 | WHERE, WHEN AND HOW

*There is a time and a place for everything.*

**A. Barclay**

Places are important. We all have our favourites, places that feel good, places that we feel relaxed and happy in, places that bring back good memories of times past. But we also have places that don't feel good, that we don't feel relaxed in, places that remind us of unhappy or stressful events from the past, places that just don't feel 'right'. The place that you use for your negotiation is important, and getting it right – choosing the right place – is just as significant as all the other bits of the preparation that you've done so far.

Just think about it. So far, you've worked hard on your preparation. You've set your objectives, assessed the other side, reviewed and agreed your strategy and tactics. But all of this could be wasted, could go down the pan – unless you get the environment of your negotiation right. But, as you'll see later in this chapter, the environment isn't the only thing that you need to get right. For you also need to make sure that you've thought through two other important factors: the timing and pace that you want your negotiation to follow; and, just as important, the 'how' or style of that negotiation. Let's start by looking at what you need to bear in mind as you chose the place of your negotiation.

## Yours or mine?

One of the first questions that you face about the 'where' of your negotiation is one that's concerned with ownership. 'Yours or mine?' or, to put it another way, 'Home or away?' – that's the question. There are, of course, negotiating situations in which circumstances take this choice out of your hands. For example, when you're negotiating over the price of the freezer or cold box that you prepared for in the last chapter, it is very unlikely that you'll be doing that on your home ground. You'll be in a store, on the sales floor, probably standing by the display model. In other words, you'll be playing away, you'll be on the salesperson's home turf. But even so, as you'll soon see, there are actions that you can take to either adjust that situation or to limit its disadvantages. Let's take a look at the pros and cons of the Home and the Away locations.

Home is where you:

>  have more control than the other side
>
>  are familiar with the location
>
>  have ready access to support in the form of people or documents
>
>  get to choose the space – that is the office, board room or conference room – that you use
>
>  can arrange the room layout to your advantage
>
>  can arrange for strategic interruptions
>
>  might have to suffer unplanned interruptions.

Away is what it says – it is away from your home. But that away can be either:

>  the other side's home ground, or
>
>  a neutral ground that's away to both of you and home to neither.

Let's look at the other side's home ground first. Their home ground is where you:

>  have less control than they do
>
>  only have direct and ready access to the support that you bring with you
>
>  have little influence on the space that you use
>
>  are unfamiliar with the location
>
>  have to accept the room layout as it is
>
>  can arrange strategic interruptions by saying, for example, that you need to check a point made with somebody back in head office

■ will have to suffer their planned and unplanned interruptions.

When we look at the ground that is away for both of you – the neutral ground – we find that:

■ neither of you will be familiar with the location
■ both you and the other side will have to bring your back-up and support systems with you
■ the choice of space used and its layout can be a point of discussion and early agreement between you and the other side
■ interruptions can be kept at bay.

If you decide that you are going the neutral ground route, then do make sure that it is really neutral. There is nothing worse than thinking you booked a conference room in a hotel that is neutral and then finding that the other side is a frequent visitor and on first name terms with most of the hotel's staff.

We've already seen that in some negotiating situations the choice of what location you use is out of your hands. If this happens then you have to accept the situation but you can either do all you can to reduce its disadvantages for you or stake a claim in a bit of their territory. For example, before you start detailed negotiations with the freezer salesperson, tell them that you'd like to discuss a possible deal – but isn't there somewhere more private where you could talk – like his or her office.

---

### THE TEST DRIVE

A test drive is a must when you're about to deal over your new car – you should never buy a new car without having driven it for at least 20 miles. Apart from getting to know the car you can also use the test drive as a way of staking a claim on a bit of the other side's territory – the new car. Get them to pick you up at – and bring you back to – your home and then do the dealing over a cup of tea (or coffee) in your lounge.

Wherever it is, the place that you negotiate in should be one:
- that you feel mentally and physically comfortable in
- where you can clearly hear – without interruption – all that's said
- that has all the facilities that you need – such as chairs, flip chart boards, audio visual aids, etc.
- that has or is close to overnight stay facilities – if you need them, and finally,
- that's private and adequately secure so that your negotiations can be conducted in private.

## Negotiating space

Space, somebody once said, is the final frontier. But, as far as your negotiation is concerned, it's the first frontier. The ways that you use the space around you when you negotiate are as individual, distinctive and particular as you are. We all, for example, have what is known as a 'personal space'. This space is roughly circular in shape with us occupying an off-centre position – with more personal space to our front than to our rear. This size of this circle depends upon our personality, age, gender and status. It is also influenced by the situation that we're in – such as whether we like or dislike the people around us. The way that we use this and other parts of the space around us sends signals to the people around us. For example, if you wish to control a meeting then the best place to sit is at the head of the table or, if there isn't a table, in the chair which is largest or occupies a key position in the room. The distances that we keep or allow between us and other people are eloquent about how we feel about them. For example, most of the informal conversations that you'll have – like those that might occur on the fringes of our negotiations – take place with a distance of half a metre to $1^{1}/_{4}$ metres between you and the person you're talking to. In the more formal part of your negotiation this separation distance can rise to as high as $3^{1}/_{2}$ metres. As a consequence you'll have to speaker louder, supplement your words with gestures or facial expressions and signal which person you're talking (or listening) to by the direction of your gaze. The way that you use these non-verbal ways of communicating is important – as you'll see in Chapter 6. In negotiations that involve large teams, separation distances can rise to as high as $7^1/_2$ metres. At this sort of distance you'll have to use emphasized vocal cues, posture and gestures to replace the eye contact and facial expression that you used when you were closer to each other. Status can also influence this separation distance with high status individuals needing – or being given – more and better protected space. But status isn't the only factor that influences the way that you use your negotiating space. You'll sit or stand closer to the people that you like, are similar to or need approval from and you'll sit or stand further away from those that you dislike or think of as being somehow 'different'. All of these factors influence the ways in which you'll use and arrange the spaces of your negotiation.

## Which seat is yours?

Many, but not all, of your negotiations will be conducted while you are seated. When you sit you adopt a posture that's half-way between the extremes of lying down and standing up. When you sit down with someone, you signal your social availability to them. Sitting with someone means you are accessible to them; you can see, touch and hear each other. This sitting together can be informal, as when you talk to your friends or when you eat breakfast together with your family, or formal, as when you sit with your boss to be told whether or not you've got a pay rise this year. What you intend to do when you sit together and the way that you intend to do it influences the seating arrangement that you choose. For example, the corner seating arrangement is the most informal. In this, you're close to the other person, you can see and touch them as well as being able to see their papers or notes. While sitting side by side is less informal, it is usually seen as a seating arrangement that is co-operative. It is easy, for example, to compare or exchange written material in this position. But when you're in competition with or unsure about someone, then you almost always choose to sit opposite to them. You do this so that you can see and watch what they're doing. Many of your formal negotiations will adopt this 'sitting opposite' seating arrangement. The opposing teams will face each other across a rectangular table with the team leaders seated opposite to each other. But in really big negotiations – such as those between several opposing groups – the people present are often limited to the representatives of those groups and are seated in a large circle or at a circular table. What happens at these negotiations is often controlled by a chairperson – who has to act impartially – and speakers may even have to get up to go to a stand or podium to make their case.

But you don't have to use rectangular tables, nor do you have to abide by the 'sitting opposite' arrangement. For example, you and the other side can sit at a round table or even at no table at all, and you don't have to sit in opposition to each other – you can mix the two teams up by sitting them adjacent to each other. Whatever you decide to do about the seating arrangements for your negotiation it is worth making sure that:

- the seats that you use are comfortable
- the people on your team that you need to check or consult with are seated near you
- the person from the other side with whom you have the most conflict or difficulty with is seated near to or opposite to you – so that you can make eye contact with them
- you can make eye contact with the key people in both your team and theirs.

# Timing and pace

The 'when' and 'how' of your negotiation – its timing and pace – can have a considerable effect upon its outcome. For example, if you're in a negotiation about an issue that has blown up suddenly or about which there are strong feelings, then it is worth trying to slow down the pace of these negotiations. Doing this can be tricky, particularly if you don't want to be seen as wasting time or being obstructive. But it is worthwhile. Decisions made under the influence of high feelings often have to be reviewed and even revised when the passage of time and oncoming calm reveal other or different facts and views. But there can also be situations that need a speedy and effective response on your part. Let's assume, for example, that in your negotiation, the other side presents a case that is particularly clear-cut and strong – one that you know you'll accept. Most negotiating pundits would argue that, in circumstances like this, it is wrong to give in too soon; you must make the other side work for their gains. But I would argue that you'll gain more by agreeing, quickly and cheerfully. Doing that will actually strengthen – rather than weaken – your relationship with the other side. You'll gain respect and be seen as a negotiator who is not only effective, but also fair. All of which brings us round to the final issue of this chapter – the issue of what style that you'll adopt in your negotiation.

## Style

Someone, somewhere, once said that style is 'how what is done is done'. The choice that you face, in choosing what style you'll adopt in your negotiations, is enormous. You can be anything you want to be – dramatic or reserved, animated or inexpressive, relaxed or frenetic, open or closed, friendly or hostile or, as you'll see in Chapter 7, aggressive or passive. But if choosing the style for your negotiations is one thing then sustaining it – sometimes in the face of considerable pressure – is quite another. For this reason, it is sensible to choose a style that you are comfortable with. If you're part of a negotiating team, you've more latitude with the issue of style than you may have realized. The sensible way to exploit this is to give your team mates roles that reflect and are compatible with their natural styles. For example, it is unwise to ask or expect someone with a naturally expressive face to be 'poker-faced' – and expect them to sustain that 'poker-face' for long. For the majority of us the style that works is one that's close to our natural one; it's the one that feels 'right' and that you can sustain without undue strain. That style – your style – involves the Three Cs. For when we use it, we are:

- ■ Considered
- ■ Careful, and
- ■ Calm

The first two of these – Considered and Careful – have their roots in your preparation. They follow, logically and as surely as night follows day, from that preparation. After all, if you've done it well, you know:

- more than the other side
- what they are likely to do
- what they want to achieve.

You'll also be clear about:

- want you want to achieve
- how you're going to do that.

All of this means that you're almost ready. But the third of these Cs – Calm – is one that starts with the knowledge that you've done your preparation – and done it well – and, as you'll now see, finds completion in a simple but easy series of steps: steps that are to do with the way that you prepare yourself for your negotiation.

## Being relaxed

The first step towards being calm is about being relaxed. Relaxation is an unusual state to be in. It isn't about going all limp and floppy; it's actually a dynamic adaptive state balanced between arousal and repose. There are all sorts of ways of getting into that state and the trick is to find one that works for you.

Try this one to start with:

---

**GETTING RELAXED**

First, tense your body – clench your fists, curl up you feet and toes, make a face.

Hold that tension for a few moments – notice how it feels.

Then exhale, let it go – completely – and relax, let go of the tensions.

Now tense your body again – only half as much as the first time.

Hold it, recognize it, feel the pull of your muscles.

Then exhale, let it go, relax, feel the warmth of your body.

Now tense your body again – only half as much as the last time.

Hold it, feel the subtle pulls and twists in your back and neck.

Then exhale; let it go, relax.

Now tense only your mind, let it clasp around your fear of the coming negotiation, feel the pain of that fear.

Then breathe, let yourself be free, drop that pain.

---

You can use this – or something like it – in the car, in the train, on the bus or in the quiet of a private space as you're waiting to go into your negotiation. It doesn't take long and the more you use it, the better you'll get at it! With practice you'll be able to get into a quiet and focused state – one that, as you'll see in Chapter 7, enables you to be a Cool Negotiator – one who is assertive rather than aggressive, one who stands up for your own rights without 'violating' another's rights.

## Being comfortable

The second step towards being calm is about being comfortable. You can feel comfortable for a number of reasons. For example, I feel at my most comfortable when I'm in bed – after a hard but worthwhile day – and just before I go to sleep. You may feel comfortable when, on a balmy summer evening, you're sitting in your garden, cool drink in hand. But those sorts of 'comfortable' aren't what you're looking for. What you need is the sort of comfortable that means you're at ease but not 'over easy'. It is the sort of comfortable that means that you're relaxed but also, as they say, 'ready, willing and able'.

Two of the most significant contributors to this sort of comfortable are to do with making sure that you are alert and feel good.

Being alert follows on from being well rested, and being well rested follows on from getting a good night's sleep. If it is a big negotiation, travel the day before and make sure that you get a comfortable room in a good hotel. There's nothing worse than arriving in the negotiating room straight from a two- or three-hour journey. You'll be over-stressed after such a journey and being over-stressed means you won't perform at your best. That journey also probably means that the way that you look has lost the clean sharp edge that it had before you set out. As we'll see in the next chapter, our appearance – the clothes that we wear, the way we do our hair, the make-up, jewellery and watches that we wear – all of these give other people clues about us. They often adjust their behaviour towards us as a result of these clues. The important thing here is not that you must wear a business suit or even a tie – it is that you look clean and tidy and are wearing clothes that are comfortable and appropriate. 'Appropriate' might mean anything from jeans to suits and in-between – it all depends who you're negotiating with. But the one thing that you can be sure of is that clothes that distract the other side aren't appropriate.

## What next?

In the next chapter you'll look at one of the key features of your negotiating – being able to communicate effectively with the other side

## Checklist ☑

In this chapter you have looked at the environment, timing and style of your negotiations. You have seen that:

negotiations can take place in:

- – your space, or ☐
- – the other side's space, or ☐
- – a neutral space. ☐

each of these have its advantages and disadvantages. ☐

the ways we use and arrange those spaces are important. ☐

the timing, pace and style of your negotiating can make major contributions to its outcomes. ☐

the style that works best is one that's close to your natural one. ☐

that style uses the Three Cs:

- – Considered ☐
- – Careful ☐
- – Calm. ☐

All of these have their roots in your preparation, but being Calm also means being:

- – alert ☐
- – relaxed ☐
- – comfortable. ☐

# 6 PREPARING YOURSELF – COMMUNICATION SKILLS

*When the eyes say one thing, and the tongue another, a practised man relies on the language of the first.*

**Emerson**

Being able to communicate effectively is something that's vital to the negotiating process. Seems obvious doesn't it? Yet most of us aren't good communicators. We get by with some sort of shuffle in the dance of communication. We miss our targets more often than we hit them and we often stand, perplexed and amazed, when others fail to understand what we've said or written. There's no reason to feel ashamed if this describes how you have felt. It is a common malady – I've felt it, you've felt it, we've all felt it. As a species we seem to get it wrong in the communication stakes more often than we get it right.

But this needn't be so! For good, effective, focused communication can be learnt and when it has, the results are impressive. Have you noticed how great communicators stand out from the crowd? They know about the how and when of saying it, even down to the pauses, inflections and the 'right' tone of voice to use. But effective communication isn't just about the way you say it – it is also about *what* you say. It is about just enough and no more, about concision and brevity. Learning all of this – knowing what to say and how to say it – is important in your negotiation. If you can do that then you'll not only know more than the person you're negotiating with, you'll also know how and when to communicate that to maximum effect! When you do this, you'll not only have the upper hand – no matter how good the other side is – you'll also have a sure-fire ticket to success.

But becoming an effective communicator – making that vital shift from 'hit or miss' to 'hitting the target every time' – doesn't happen overnight. You'll need to take time out, to prepare your words – spoken or written – to sharpen their approach, to make sure their aim and focus are clear and precise. You'll need, in short, to prepare and train yourself for your communication just as surely as if you were running in the Boston or the London Marathon.

# Why and what

We all need to communicate. You should have little doubt about this. For when you talk or write you make your needs known, find out what you want to know or declare your intentions in war, love or anger. In the work-a-day world you communicate – or, at least, try to – with an enormously wide range of people. Customers, colleagues, bosses, team-mates, inspectors, union representatives, delivery people – the list goes on and on. You need to communicate with each and every one of them, and to do so effectively and clearly. Outside of the workplace it is just the same, except now it's shopkeepers, dentists, doctors, hairdressers, supermarket people, traffic wardens, police people, partners, lovers or children – the list is even bigger – that you communicate with. And, just as was so in the workplace, you need to communicate effectively.

But what is it that you communicate and why do you do it? The list of answers to these questions is just as long, if not longer, than those you've seen above. For you do it in order to persuade, inform, instruct, cajole, interest, ask, interrogate or even seduce the people that you work, play, shop, love or live with. In order to do this effectively you need skills. But these aren't just any old skills – they're the skills that mean you can write and speak fluently, the skills that mean you can use these effectively to present information, facts and feelings. But you aren't alone in your need to communicate – others need to communicate with you. This means that you also need the skills of being able to hear and listen, you need to be able to receive and respond to the information, facts and feelings that they send to you.

But do you always achieve all of that? No, of course you don't. In order to find out why this is so, you need to look at some of the basics of this curious process called communication.

# Back to basics

If you look in *Webster's* or the *Oxford English Dictionary*, you'll find communication described as something that involves the actions of imparting, bestowing and revealing to others. When you delve further in these and other tomes you'll find that communication is about:

■ passing information, and

■ using previously agreed symbols – such as words and numbers – to do so.

But you know that that's not all that communication's about. Your own experience tells you, for example, that you also communicate when you praise, express displeasure or state your opinions and that you do it when you say something a simple as 'Hello' to your friends or neighbours. If you think about it, you'll soon see that communication casts a wide net – it goes a lot further than just passing information. For you communicate about:

■ 'hard' stuff such as facts and figures, data or information

■ 'soft' stuff such as sentiments, feelings and emotions

■ 'you and me' stuff such as opinions, ideas and notions, and

■ 'all of us' stuff such standards, values and beliefs.

Most of these will appear – as you'll see later in this book – in the ways and means of your negotiation. Your experience also tells you that communication – like your negotiations – takes place in a wide variety of situations. It takes place when one person talks to another, when individuals address groups, crowds or audiences of people, when one group or crowd of people meets another group or when several people in a group talk together. It happens when people talk, write or wave to each other. All in all, it is a pretty flexible process – but one that, as we all know to our cost, can go wrong.

# One-way or two-way?

One of the most basic and frequent mistakes that most of us make about our communication is to assume that it is all right to make it a one-way process. This can happen when you're busy or preoccupied, when you tell someone to do something or when you say something to somebody without waiting for or caring about their response. But if you're going to be effective in your communication there are very, very, few situations in which one-way communication is acceptable. You can almost list them on the fingers of one hand – like when you shout when you see a friend is about to step off the kerb in front of a car or when you see your child about to pick up a hot plate. Outside of these few circumstances, effective communication can never be a one-way process. It has to be, if it's going to work, a two-way process, however it is undertaken.

But, you might say, there are circumstances in which you tell people to do something – like the famous 'Go clear up your room' message we send to our teenage children – and don't need, want or even get an answer. But the reality is that when you do this – that is, issue instructions – the person you're talking to is giving you feedback. This feedback doesn't have to be in words; it can be contained in the expression on their face or in his or her body posture – these tell you something. They tell you whether your message has been heard and understood; they tell you what they feel about that message or you. What goes on looks something like Figure 6.1.

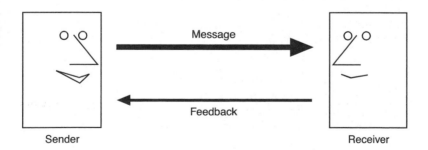

**Figure 6.1  Communication**

# Full or partial?

But if your communication is going to be about more than grunts or nods, then this feedback will need to change. It needs to contain more information, often as much as or even more than the original message. When this happens both the feedback and the original message are able to convey information, ideas and feelings. This shift is an important one – it's what the theorists call the shift from *partial* communication to *full* communication – and it takes real skill and experience to be able to do it consistently. Real full communication is actually quite rare and most of your (or my) communications don't reach its high plateau. But when it does happen, this is often because you and the person you're communicating with have:

■ shared concerns, goals or objectives

■ adequate trust in each other, and

■ a shared commitment to the generation of a future outcome that's mutually acceptable.

Don't be surprised if this sounds familiar. If you think about it for a moment, you'll realize that in Chapter 1 you saw that negotiation helps you to identify decisions that are also acceptable to all involved and are also about the what and how of your future actions. Now that you can begin to see how effective, full communication fits into your negotiating, you need to probe further into the ways and means of your communications.

# How do we do it?

Communication, and particularly 'Full Communication', isn't quite as simple as it has been shown to be so far. For example, you think more than you speak and you often speak more than you write. You often have thoughts that are not communicated to others and when you do communicate them – in speech or writing – then you often limit or edit what you say or write. When you speak and write you do so with words and in a style that you think are appropriate – to the subject, the circumstances, the person who's listening or reading and the relationship that you have with them.

All of this is wrapped up in a process that is often called 'encoding'. A simple and limited example of encoding would be your choosing to use technical words when you are talking about a technical subject and when you know that the person that you're talking or writing to understands them. That is, you translate your selected thoughts into appropriate words. When the person to whom you're talking or writing hears or reads the words, then the reverse process takes place. That is he or she converts that speech or text from words into his or her own set of ideas or thoughts. This, not surprisingly, is called 'decoding'.

What goes on during the thoughts and words of these conversions is complex and not fully understood. But it is evident that it does enable you to tap into the associations that some of your words have for you. Words like 'love' or 'mother', for example, are associated in your mind with a whole raft of experiences from your past. These experiences colour the ways in which you react to those words and your reactions can be positive and good or negative and bad. Choosing your words carefully and using these associations well is important in your negotiation. The ease (or difficulty) with which you do all of this depends partly upon your ability to 'decode'. Whether you've met and understood the sorts of words used, or even the language that they are spoken or written in, can help or hinder the ease with which you do (or don't) understand the message. But the content of the message and the way that it is delivered are also important.

# The 'write' words

Communicating and negotiating have much in common – they both have to be prepared with care and attention. The preparation for communication involves you in choosing, with care, the what and how of what you say or write. Getting this right is a key step towards becoming an effective communicator. This preparation should, for example, take into account all that you know about the people that you're talking to, including, for example, their language and language skills, whether they are physically near or distant, whether they are directly accessible and their likely reaction to your message. For example, there is little point in using phrases like *habeas corpus* if the person you're writing or talking to hasn't met them before or doesn't understand what they mean. Remember that most professions have their own vocabulary of 'technical' words – or jargon – and to the outsider these are often baffling and difficult to understand.

But using the right words isn't all that needs to be taken into account – you also have to consider the *way* the message is sent. The influence of this can be considerable and you have to choose carefully both the *medium* of your communication (as in the spoken or written word) and the *channel* through which it passes (as in a book, note, telephone call or film).

Experience will tell you that there are some messages that are better spoken than written and there are other messages that are better written than spoken. The reasons for this include the message's contents, its confidentiality, the likely reaction of the receiver and a future need to be able to prove what was sent and when it was sent. For example, if you sack or discipline someone, you'll make sure that whatever you say in the face-to-face interview is confirmed in writing – thus providing a record for the future. But if you want to test whether one of your staff was interested in a transfer to the London office, you'll have an informal face-to-face discussion with them. If that isn't possible – because she's in Paris and you're in New York – you'll ring her up and talk to her on the telephone. The important thing here is to choose both the *medium* of your communications and its *channel* so that the message will be received – and understood. If you get either of these wrong, then your message might be misunderstood or not even arrive at all.

---

### TO WRITE OR NOT TO WRITE?

Jane had to tell her team about the new product launch date. How should she do it?

'Writing a note would be best,' she thought. It was quick, easy and told them all at the same time. 'But,' she told herself, 'it was vital that the date shouldn't leak to their competitor.'

What would you do?

# Hue and cry

Most of your communications take place in the real world, a world that's noisy, busy and full of people who are often preoccupied with their own affairs. As a consequence, even when you use appropriate words, the 'right' *channel* and the correct *medium*, it doesn't necessarily mean that your messages will get through. You might, for example, find yourself trying to talk in a crowded and noisy restaurant or having to shout over the traffic noise coming in through the open windows of a too-hot conference room. Your messages may be misheard because of a bad telephone connection or misread because of a bad fax copy or a misspelled text.

But not all of the noise and interference is external. You might be preoccupied with other issues, have a headache or not like the person who is speaking or writing to you. If you're going to be sure that you'll be able to communicate well and clearly in your negotiation, then you must either eliminate these external and internal factors or else find a way of communicating that isn't susceptible to them.

# Ways and means

Almost all of your negotiations will use the spoken word. It is flexible and direct. It can be used formally or informally, at length or briefly and in a manner which reflects your feelings and your own personal style. Your spoken words can be recorded, transmitted as spoken over long distances by radio or telephone and used to communicate with groups or individuals. When you speak to people it can:

- make them feel that they've been personally consulted
- lead to expression of feelings as well as ideas
- enable sharing and comparing.

When you can see each other your spoken words are complemented and supported by what is often called 'body language'. This language that our bodies speak is an eloquent one. We all use it. We wave, point, smile or frown at each other. We gesture with our hands, fold our arms, scratch our noses, pull our ears, cross our legs and lean towards – or away from – each other. The clothes that we wear, the way we do our hair, the make-up, jewellery and watches that we wear all add to its messages. The power and diversity of this language are considerable. It will have dominated your face-to-face communications – particularly when these involved feelings and emotions – since you were a small child. Most of our facial expressions are about expressing these emotions and these provide as much as half of the 'meaning' of any face-to-face communication. But facial expressions, gestures and movements don't just act on their own – they also complement, supplement and add emphasis to the words that we speak. Being able to understand and use this body language is important. For without that understanding you are blind to a major and significant part of the messages that you are sent. With it you will be able to read and respond to the whole of those messages. However, your use and awareness of body language is often not conscious. You might, for example, find yourself unable to explain why you did or didn't trust someone – while a less involved observer might find the answer 'writ large' in their body language. Understanding and being able to use this non-verbal way of communicating can make a significant difference to the way you will negotiate.

---

### BODY LANGUAGE CHECKOUT

Next time you watch a play, drama or video on TV, try turning the sound off. Concentrate on the facial expressions and gestures used and see if you can follow what's going on. Look out for answers to questions such as:

■ Who's in charge of whom?

or

■ Who's not telling the truth?

---

## Writ large or small?

We rarely negotiate by using the written word. It can, however, make a major contribution to the ways in which we record our agreements and present them to the outside world. The main reason for its limited use is its indirect nature. To negotiate successfully, you need the interplay of the spoken word. The written word does, however, have its advantages. It can, for example, enable you to express your own ideas and feelings without having to respond to other people's reactions and responses. Its indirectness will enable you to put more thought into your choice of words and your written messages can be reshaped until satisfactory. As with the spoken word, the written communication can be brief or lengthy, formal or informal and also, for the experienced writer, can reflect an individual style. The tangible form of the written word means that it can:

■ be easily copied and so provide physical evidence of transmission and content

■ be sent to a number of people at the same time.

In the end, whatever the ways and means of your communication, good negotiating needs good communication.

# What next?

In the next chapter you'll look at how being assertive – rather than aggressive or passive – can help you negotiate.

# Checklist ✔

In this chapter you have seen that:

■ most of us could communicate better ☐

■ effective, focused communication:

  – can be learnt ☐

  – is a two-way dynamic process ☐

  – requires thought and planning ☐

  – involves the choice of the 'right' medium and channel. ☐

■ effective communication will only happen if you've thought through and done something about:

  – needs of the people you're communicating with ☐

  – what might cause it to fail. ☐

■ most negotiations use the spoken word.                    ☐
■ the words that you speak are a direct and flexible way
   of communicating.                                                ☐
■ the words you speak are complemented and supported
   by your 'body language'.                                        ☐
■ your gestures, facial expressions, movements,
   postures, gaze and appearance are all part of your body
   language.                                                            ☐
■ good negotiating needs good communication.          ☐

# 7 | PREPARING YOURSELF – GETTING ASSERTIVE

*Nobody can give you freedom.*

**Malcolm X**

You've already seen – perhaps even experienced – how conflict is woven into the warp and weft of your negotiations. It's core to them – however they start and whatever they're about. After all, conflict is the reason why you need to negotiate. It's also the engine, the driving force, that can – if you let it – spin your negotiation through to a successful conclusion. Conflict, as we all know, raises its head whenever and wherever what we want collides with what other people want.

Let's take a look at some typical work-a-day conflicts:

- your boss asks you to work late on the evening of your wedding anniversary – when you've arranged to go out to dinner with your wife or husband.
- you're faced with an irate customer who's being rude – but whose business you don't want to lose.
- you disagree with your director – a forceful driving ambitious young man who must have his own way.
- you've been told to tell your staff about a senior management decision that you don't agree with.

All of these are conflict situations. They all possess the potential, if not the actuality, for a real down-and-out, shouting and door-slamming row. Most of us find these situations very uncomfortable; they make us anxious, stressed, uneasy. You, like everybody else, will feel that you're faced with the sort of fight-or-flight situation that our ancestors faced when they came face to face with a sabre tooth tiger. Either you fight, stand up for your rights, or you back down, give in. Which would you do?

Before you answer that question, I think you ought to know that it isn't quite as simple as that, or as black and white as I've painted it. It isn't just a choice between the two extremes of fighting or giving in. There's another way – a middle way – the way of assertion.

## Assertion

Assertion hasn't always had a good press. In its early days, being assertive was seen by many people as being about trumpeting your own rights, wants and desires – and doing so at the cost of other people's. But time and a changing world have mellowed this perspective and it is now seen differently. One of the easiest ways to find out about this view of assertion is to find out what it isn't.

Assertion isn't, for example, about aggression. The popular dictionary definitions for aggressive behaviour are 'unprovoked attacks', 'eagerness to quarrel' and 'threatening'. People who are aggressive are seen as wanting to force their wishes on others, to overpower these other people in order to get what they want. This need to be dominant, to ensure that your needs are fulfilled – and that other people's aren't – seems to be typical of aggression. Aggressive negotiators are very competitive. They use conflict as a lever, they adopt the Competition style of conflict management – a style that, as we saw in Chapter 1, is also called the win–lose style. They win – and to do that they make sure that others lose. All of this is very different from being assertive.

But if assertion and aggression are different, then what about the other behavioural extreme – being passive or submissive? This sort of behaviour is the opposite of aggression. For when we behave submissively, we accept that other people's needs, views and rights are paramount and that our needs, views and rights are unimportant or insignificant. We saw this sort of behaviour in another of the Five Basics of Conflict Management (Chapter 1) – the one called the Accommodation style. When we use this way of managing conflict, we accommodate the needs of others by giving in, by surrendering. That is why it is also called the 'Submit and Comply' style. Negotiators who use this style never get their needs answered – because they're too busy answering other people's needs. Again, all of this is very different from being assertive.

So if assertion isn't about being aggressive and it isn't about being passive – then what is it about? The answer comes if you look at the range of ways we behave as being a spectrum – one that has aggression and submission at its opposite and extreme ends. After all, this fits with your experience and it reflects that fact that aggression and submission are complete opposites. When you do this, you'll soon realize that between these two extremes there lies a wide range of ways of behaving. In the middle of this we find assertion. Let's see if this gets any clearer in the following situation.

---

**WHAT NOW?**

Joe was about half way through writing the report when the phone rang. He hesitated – the report needed to be finished today – but then picked up the phone. It was Mark, his boss – who told Joe he wanted him to stand in for him at the Safety Committee meeting that afternoon. 'It's the wife's birthday,' Mark said, 'I'm taking her out for lunch.' Joe hesitated, remembering all the other times when Mark had pulled a stunt like this. 'I'll see you right' he used to say – but never did. The report lay in front of him – unfinished. It was about his special project and it was due at the Executive Committee meeting next week. 'OK then Joe?' – Mark's voice seemed to boom in Joe's ear. What should he do – tell Mark where to get off or give in as usual? There must be another way!

Here are some examples of that other way – the 'middle way':

| SITUATION | RESPONSES | | |
|---|---|---|---|
| | **PASSIVE** | **ASSERTIVE** | **AGGRESSIVE** |
| **1.** A man lights up a cigarette in a non-smoking section of a train. | Say nothing and do nothing. Suffer in silence. | Point to the non-smoking sign and ask him to stop. | Get angry and threaten to call the guard. |
| **2.** Your boss asks you to attend an after hours meeting on the evening of your wedding anniversary celebration. | Say that you'll attend but without saying anything about your celebration. | Tell him of your celebration and that normally you'd like to help out – but not tonight. | Respond with anger, saying that he always picks on you and you have had enough. |
| **3.** One of your staff is openly and unfairly critical of you in a meeting with an important client. | Say nothing and allow the client to think that the criticism is valid. | Tell him/her that you are surprised by the comments and would like to discuss his/her feelings at a more appropriate time. | Tell him/her that he/she doesn't know what he/she is talking about and should shut up. |
| **4.** Your secretary has produced an unsatisfactory letter with spelling mistakes and omissions. | 'I wonder if you could spare the time to change a few things?' | 'I'd like you to do this letter again. I have marked the mistakes that you made.' | 'Why is it that you can't type a decent letter?' |

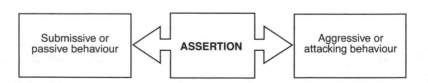

**Figure 7.1  Ways of behaving**

# Rights

By now you should be able to see that if there's one thing that stands out about being assertive, then it is the act of standing up for your rights. But what are your or my rights and how do we get them?

The answer is that we all, as human beings, have rights. This isn't a new thing. The human rights issue has been with us for a long time, even if not all our leaders were, or for that matter still are, prepared to recognize these rights. For many of us these rights are so basic, so interwoven in the fabric of our lives, that we almost take them for granted. They include things like the right to:

■ have and express your own opinions
■ expect your views and opinions to count – rather than be ignored
■ have your own individual set of wants and needs – and to be able to strive to have these answered in ways that are satisfying and meaningful for you
■ follow whatever religion you want to follow
■ make mistakes.

But you and everybody who has a job also have another set of rights. These – our employment rights – are there because of the legislation that our governments have enacted. These tell you what you have a right to expect in your place of work. They cover issues like how warm it should or shouldn't be in your places of work, what hours you should work, how you should be protected from dangerous equipment or fumes, whether you should have a formal contract of employment and whether you can have maternity (or paternity) leave. Other place-of-work rights are there because your employer has granted them in order to make working for them attractive. These are often spelt out in your employment contract or in the employee's handbook that you are given when you join the company. These rights are often specific to your employer and don't have the full force of the law behind them – except when they're a part of your contract of employment. They might include, for example, the right to:

■ be a member of the company pension scheme

- take sabbatical leave
- use a company flat at the seaside for your family holiday
- take time off, with pay, to study for relevant qualifications.

The third and last group of workplace rights aren't so easy to pin down. These are the rights that we have because of the culture of our organizations. The simplest way of defining this culture is to say that it is 'how things are done around here'. This means that these 'cultural' rights aren't formal written-down rights – they're rights that you have because, as they say, that's the way things are done here. They can come about because of the relationship that you have with your boss or the views that a senior manager might have about what makes people 'tick'. They often make the difference between a happy team and an unhappy one but, because of their nature, they can be eroded or undermined quite easily. The introduction of a new boss can quickly mean that 'we don't do things that way any more'. The range of these rights is enormous but typical examples would be:

- being able to say 'no' to requests that you think are unreasonable – without being penalized or punished
- being able to criticize poor performance – irrespective of whose it is
- getting credit for above average work
- being able to expect good work from your staff
- being involved in decisions that affect you or your work area.

But none of these rights are going to help you unless you, and those around you, acknowledge that you have them. Once that takes place the next step that you can take towards being effectively assertive in your negotiation is to recognize that you don't just have rights, you also have responsibilities.

## Responsibilities

Responsibilities aren't in short supply. We're all responsible to somebody for something. We're all, for example, responsible for making sure that we drive our cars safely and at reasonable speeds. If we fail to do that, and get caught in a speed trap, then we face prosecution by the police. As parents we are responsible for making sure that our children attend school and for their emotional and physical well-being. Here are some examples of the workplace responsibilities you might have:

- making sure that those who work for or with you have the freedom to say what they want – to express their views and ideas
- using your time and creativity productively
- abiding by the rules and regulations of your workplace.

When you compare some of these responsibilities with the rights that were identified earlier, you soon begin to see that there's trouble ahead. For example, your right to express your own opinions and to have them count could act against your responsibility for making sure that those who work for or with you can also express their views and ideas. I'm sure you can think of other examples – it's the classic struggle between your rights, wants and needs and those of others. So how do you solve it? The key lies in the balance that you achieve between your rights and your responsibilities.

# The right balance

Getting this balance right is important. If you can do that, then you can start to find those reasonable working compromises that go to make your and other people's lives liveable. But that's not all that you'll find, for finding the 'right' balance between your responsibilities and your rights takes the sting out of 'it's my right'-dominated assertions and turns them into workable, yet powerful, opportunities for negotiated compromise. It is a balance that recognizes, for example, that while you have the right to criticize other people's poor performance in the workplace, you also have the responsibility to acknowledge their right to make mistakes. In that reasonable balance you'll need to recognize that there may be quite legitimate and acceptable reasons for what you see as poor performance – such as ill health, lack of information or lack of training.

In short, this sort of 'balanced' assertiveness involves 'standing up' for one's own rights without 'violating' another's rights. Achieving this will involve you in:

■ learning how to use your assertiveness skilfully
■ being effective in your communications and using both the  verbal and non-verbal ways of doing that
■ taking the risk that your assertiveness may not produce the  result you desire, and
■ exercising your judgement about when and where you use that assertiveness.

One of the situations in which being assertive can make a valuable contribution is at the stressful negotiating table.

## Negotiations and stress

Negotiating and stress go hand-in-hand. You're anxious that you will lose; you don't want to be 'taken for a ride' or 'ripped off' by an aggressive and manipulative opponent who's out to get his or her needs answered at your expense. You'll get upset, frustrated, put out if you don't get what you want. Even when things are going well, you can feel frustrated because the other side is slow to respond to your proposals or because they are unable or unwilling to acknowledge or recognize the compromises that you're making. All of these emotions are perfectly natural. After all, you're a human being and human beings do have feelings.

But having these feelings can lead, almost without you being aware of it, to you losing control of your negotiation. For when you're stimulated in these ways – when, as they say, your buttons get pressed – it can easily lead to you becoming angry. And when you get angry you start that slow insidious slide down the slope that leads to failure. Some of us (me included!) have short fuses, we react quickly and then subside just as quickly. Others have long, slow burn times that terminate in explosions of words and actions that last for quite a while. It doesn't matter which you are, the result is the same. For when you lose your cool – you also lose control.

---

### SAVED BY THE BELL

It is 10.00 am on Monday morning in a small but busy advertising agency. Kate, the account manager's 'Girl Friday', is apologizing to the Managing Director – her boss, Roger, hasn't arrived for the 9.30 am meeting that he'd asked for late on Friday. This isn't the first time this has happened and the MD (who is famous for his acid tongue) is just getting into his stride. 'Kate,' he says, with a smirk writ large across his jowls, 'are you sure you're up to looking after Roger?' Kate begins to see red – after all it isn't her fault. She'd reminded Roger about the meeting last thing on Friday. She's just about to tell him where to shove his job when the telephone rings ...

---

## Cool ways

Stress – and its close cousin anger – are your body's reactions to external events. These events can be obvious and 'in your face' – such as when somebody is rude and aggressive or doesn't listen to you – or subtle and insidious – as when someone won't answer your questions or you get the feeling that someone's not being honest with you. Few of these external events are under your control – neither you nor I can make people be polite or honest. When things like this happen you start to get stressed.

So what can you do about it – how can you de-stress yourself or, better still, how can you stop yourself getting stressed in the first place? The answer, of course, lies – like the stress itself – within yourself. But it doesn't lie in ignoring your feelings. Quite the contrary, it lies in your becoming *more* aware of your feelings and emotions. You need to watch the ways in which these feelings wax and wane, you need to get better at recognizing their early onset. You need, most importantly, to find ways that enable these feelings to be used to your benefit – rather than being driven by them.

## Cool negotiation

The ways and means of your doing that lie in three simple steps – the Three S's of Cool Negotiation. These tell you that you need to:

■ Spot what's happening
■ Step away from the anger
■ Speak assertively.

Let's look at these one by one:

## Spotting what's happening

You should be able to do this easily. You won't find it a new experience. Being with someone who's getting annoyed or beginning to feel annoyed yourself is a situation that we've all been in. When it happens, when the 'temperature' of their (or your) words starts to rise, you'll be able to recognize that they (or you) start to do things like:

■ express opinions as facts – 'that won't work', 'that's a useless idea', 'that's stupid'
■ use 'I' sentences a lot – 'I think ...', 'I don't believe what you're saying', 'I don't agree'
■ push opinions at the other person – 'You should do it this way', 'You shouldn't have done that'.

Body language will also enable you to recognize that rising 'temperature' when your (or their):

■ speech becomes fluent with few hesitations and a hard, sharp, sometimes sarcastic, tone
■ gaze becomes hard and dominant trying to stare the other down
■ gestures start to be dominated by finger pointing or even fist thumping.

When the stress level of your negotiation rises, when you feel that you are beginning to lose your detachment or when you see that the other person is getting angry, then you need to take the next step – to step away, to pause.

## Stepping away

It takes skill and courage to be able to step away from a rising conflict. Most of your difficulty in doing so will come about because you'll feel that you'll 'lose face' or look stupid if you do it. But that's not all. For you'll also feel, in a very real way, the influence of the rising tide of chemicals that your body is generating in response to your feelings – feelings about being attacked, embarrassed, hurt or frightened. But if you're going to move forward then it must be done.

Every experienced negotiator has their own way of handling this – mine is to take a good deep breath and tell myself that it isn't me he or she's getting angry with, it's somebody or something in their past. Yours may be different – but finding it isn't just important, it is key to you being assertively effective in these conflicts. Once you've found it then you're ready for the next S of Cool Negotiation – that of responding, constructively and effectively, to the aggression that you face.

## Speaking assertively

There are a number of ways that you can do this. You can, for example, respond to someone who's getting angry by being emphathic, by saying things like 'I can see how angry that makes you feel' or 'It sounds like you're pretty upset about that. How can I help?' Alternatively you might want to count to four (to yourself, of course) and then respond. Whatever way you do it, it is essential that early in your response you ask for more detail or facts. This, of course, is easier said than done. It takes a brave man or woman to limit their response to an aggressively critical statement like: 'This is typical of your department – always cocking it up!' to that of a calmly said: 'What makes you say that?' This sort of response – asking for facts or clarification – usually works. But if it doesn't, even after several tries, then you might have to face the fact that your negotiation is breaking down. If that is what's happening then the best way is to cut off the discussion – but leave the door open to come back at a later date. We'll take a look at this sort of situation in more detail in Chapter 12. Right now, what you need to recognize is that being assertive can help you to steer your negotiation away from failure and into success.

## What next?

Now you have finished your preparation. In Part Two you will look at the key points and skills that you need to extend and enhance your negotiating skills.

# Checklist ✔

In this chapter you have seen that:

- conflict is core to your negotiations.                                                    ☐
- most of us find conflict very uncomfortable – it makes us anxious, stressed, uneasy.                                            ☐
- you can choose the way that you respond to this stress.                                                                                              ☐
- you can be:
  - aggressive, or                                                                                        ☐
  - submissive, or                                                                                        ☐
  - assertive.                                                                                               ☐
- effective balanced assertion involves 'standing up' for one's own rights without 'violating' another's rights.                                                                                                      ☐
- achieving this sort of assertion involves you in:
  - learning its skilful use                                                                       ☐
  - being effective in your communications                                          ☐
  - taking the risk that it may not produce the result you want                                                                                      ☐
  - exercising your judgement about when and where you use it.                                                                                        ☐
- Cool negotiating involves you in using the Three S's:
  - Spotting what's happening                                                                    ☐
  - Stepping away from the anger                                                              ☐
  - Speaking assertively.                                                                             ☐

*Part Two*

# CARRYING OUT YOUR NEGOTIATION

*In walking, just walk.*
*In sitting, just sit.*
*Above all, don't wobble.*

Yun-men

# 8 OPENING, TALKING, LISTENING AND PROPOSING

*A journey of a thousand miles must begin with a single step.*

**Chinese proverb**

Before you go any further, let's review where you've got to and what you've done so far. In Part One the key word was Preparation. You started that preparation by deciding what it was you needed – rather than wanted – from your negotiation. Then your focus shifted – you prioritized the key features of the negotiation's outcome and decided what, for you, would be its ideal value, minimum value and realistic value. Then you found out all you could about the other side, what their needs, motives and hidden agendas are, how they did it before – their negotiating history – and how they might be going to do it in your negotiation. Then you decided how you are going to do it – what the strategies and tactics of your negotiation are going to be. In the next step you reviewed the where, when and how of this negotiation – choosing its location, seating arrangements and the style you'll adopt in your negotiation. Finally, you looked at the basics of clear communication – a must for all effective negotiators – and how to use assertion, rather than aggression, in your negotiation.

Now your preparation is complete, now you're ready to move forward. In Part Two the key word is Action. It is about doing it. You'll look at how you'll do your negotiating, at the detail, the nitty-gritty, of your actions. You'll find out about the how and why of making offers, of listening to the other side's reactions, of analysing and reacting to their offers and counter-proposals and, finally, the how and why of plotting your route into and through the Bargaining Zone. Doing all of this, and doing it successfully, takes real skill, and you'll be given practical examples of how really effective negotiators do it. All of this hangs together in a framework that looks like Figure 8.1.

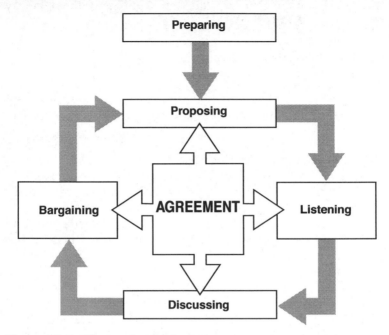

**Figure 8.1  The negotiating process**

The best place to begin all of this is as you enter the negotiating space and begin your negotiation.

# Entrances and beginnings

Entrances and beginnings are rarely easy. But creating the right atmosphere from the start is important; it is almost, but not quite, as important as the preparation that you've laboured long and hard over. To get a good beginning you need to be confident, you need to believe in yourself and what you intend to achieve. But this isn't an unconditional, arrogant sort of belief – it is one that's based on confidence. After all, you've done your preparation, you know what they want and you're clear about what you want and how you're going to try to get it. So start your negotiations the right way and do that by being:

      pleasant

      assertive, and

      firm.

Getting this right, setting the 'right' tone or atmosphere at the very beginning, is a vital step. If you get it right then you've made an important step towards agreement; if you get it wrong then you've an uphill struggle ahead of you. So, what do you do – how do you get it right?

Meeting someone is a sort of ritual. It doesn't matter if it is the first time or whether you've met them before, the rules are the same. You smile, say something appropriate and shake hands. Sounds simple doesn't it? Yes – but as some of you will have learnt to your cost, it isn't that simple. Let's take the handshake. A handshake can vary from a 'wet fish' to a 'bone-crusher'. It can be amplified by hand-clasping, forearm grasping, shoulder gripping or shoulder embracing and it can involve a hand squeeze or an up-and-down pump. In the right circumstances, all of these can be acceptable – but in the wrong circumstances any of them can lead to the other side jumping to the wrong conclusion about you as a person, and changing the way they react to you because of that. The same sort of options face you when you think about what to say when you meet. You can be formal – 'Good Morning' – or informal – 'Hi' and either of them will be acceptable in the right circumstances. But get it wrong – as in saying 'Hi' to a member of the royal family – and you're in trouble. In general, the best (and the safest) things to do are:

      enter the room with your right hand free of papers etc.

      offer a handshake early – rather than late

      shake hands firmly and briefly – without hand clasping etc.

      smile – openly but not unnecessarily

■ have good eye contact – open and level

■ listen to the other side's words of greeting and mirror
them.

Having said all of that, you do need to be aware of and sensitive to
the rules and conventions that other cultures have about touch and
greeting. In Japan, for example, handshaking is rare, and in some
Asian cultures shaking hands or any sort of physical contact
between sexes is taboo. Make sure that you've researched these
and are familiar with them before you start your negotiation. Your
objective in doing all of this is to begin the process of finding some
common ground between you and the other side.

## Common ground

The common ground that exists between you and the other side is
really important. For in it lie the dormant seeds of your agreement.
Its emergence will give you the first signals that you do have
something in common with the other side and its presence can be a
bulwark against failure when the going gets tough. This common
ground can be almost anything – your, or their, family, leisure
interests, a particular brand of motor car, a shared holiday location
or some memory or reminiscence of the last time that you met. You
do, however, need to use these with care – don't be pushy or nosy.
If you've not met them before then you should use these initial
minutes together to try to add to what you've found out about them
in your preparation. But, again, be careful – being too pushy or too
prying will create a bad impression. But you can be sure, whatever
their interests and background might be, that you do have the
following things in common with the other side:

■ a desire to reach an agreement, and

■ to do that in as pleasant a way as can be managed.

In the stress of the opening situation of your negotiation, this can
easily be forgotten or overlooked.

---

### GETTING STARTED

Mary had put her house up for sale. It was a four-bedroomed detached house in a good area. Nearby there were schools, shops and a public park.

A good family house. She'd done her homework, checked out the recent sale prices of similar houses, worked out her price range and talked to neighbours about who was the best real estate agent in the area. He'd worked hard and several couples had been to see the house. Now one of these was coming back – probably to make an offer.

Mary felt really nervous as their car drew up the drive. What should she say? What should she do? Then she remembered something her father had told her a long time ago. 'People', he'd said, 'don't like buying houses from strangers.' Then she heard the door chimes ...

---

This common ground provides you with an easy way to move on from the social pleasantries to the business of the meeting. The bridge that you use to do this is something that you've looked at in your preparation – the agenda. You'll remember that, in Chapter 4, you saw that creating a written agenda can be a powerful but potentially challenging thing to do. You also saw that one of the ways of avoiding or reducing this challenge is the draft agenda. A draft agenda – in verbal or written form – starts you talking. It looks for early agreement, it reduces the chance of surprise items, it gives you what might be your first real glimpse of the other side's 'wish list'. But, whatever else your draft agenda contains, it must – clearly and briefly – tell the other side:

- why you're here
- what you think are the things that need to be discussed
- what order you'd like to discuss them in
- what sort of time-scale you're looking at
- that you'd like their agreement to the above.

In telling them this you've made your first negotiating step – your first proposal.

# Proposals

Making a proposal is an action that you're already familiar with. Most of the time your proposals are about things like 'Let's go out for the day' or 'Let's meet up for lunch'. Sometimes they're about more important things like 'Let's buy a new house' or even 'Let's get married'. In your negotiation a proposal is always important. It is a doorway – even when in an early, tentative form – a doorway that you and the other side must use if you are to reach agreement. But if that doorway is to be used successfully then your proposal must:

■ be presented when you feel the time is right
■ be presented in a way that's clear, brief and confident
■ stress your desire to reach an agreement.

The 'right' time will depend upon what strategy you're following. Some people like to have the other side declare their hand first while others prefer to 'stake their claim' on virgin soil. Both have their advantages and disadvantages. If you're making the opening proposal then it must:

■ leave room for manoeuvre
■ indicate any conditions attached to it as in:

'If you'll give us this – we'll give you that.'

■ seek reactions as in:

'How would you feel if we offered ...'

■ NOT contain any:

– concessions
– exclusions
– unrealistic or extreme offers.

If the other side has made the opening proposal then you'll need time to consider what they've said. Don't be afraid to ask for clarification or more details – the more information you have the better. Don't feel obliged to rush in with a counter proposal – make sure you understand the what and why of their proposal before you respond. Stall or take a consultation break if you have to – but be frugal and careful in your use of these tactics. When you do respond, start with a summary of their proposal and then follow this with your response, a response that should be framed as indicated above. Remember you don't have to accept their first offer – they, like you, will have a range of values and will try to get you to sell low or buy high – at first. In all of this it's vitally important that we listen carefully to what the other side says.

# Listening

Listening is often confused with hearing. But it isn't the same. For hearing is a purely physical reaction to the noises in the air around us. As such it is an automatic, reflex-like response. You don't have to choose to hear – it happens whether you like it or not. That isn't true of your listening. For while your hearing is automatic, your listening is a deliberate and chosen action. You can chose to listen – or not listen – to someone. If you chose not to listen, then you can still hear them but you ignore or disregard what they say. If, on the other hand, you chose to listen to them then you'll be attentive to what they say; you'll focus on its sounds, content and overtones. The primary difference between listening and hearing is that your listening is active – while your hearing is reactive.

This act of listening is one of the linchpins of effective negotiation. For when you listen you not only hear the words that are spoken, you'll also hear, for example, those 'uh huh' or 'hmm' sounds that some people use to indicate that they agree and others use to show that they are listening and understanding. You'll also hear the way they speak – the pitch, tempo, loudness or softness of their words; whether they drawl, clip their words, rasp or pause. Pauses can be pregnant with meaning. They can tell you that the other person is thinking or planning or anxious or uncertain or lacking in self-confidence. The other side will also stress their spoken words, adding meaning to a sentence or focusing your attention on a particular part of it, and the pitch of their voice and the ways that it changes will tell you much about the way that they are feeling.

But listening to these words isn't the only part of the listening that you must do in your negotiation. For you must also 'listen' to the body language of the speaker. Their gestures, facial expressions and body movements can all speak to you. Gestures, for example, add emphasis to what is being said and facial expressions can give you a wealth of information – usually about what the speaker is feeling. However, if you're like most people, listening won't come easily to you.

# Effective listening

Listening effectively isn't a natural skill, but it is one that can be learnt. If you're going to succeed in your negotiations then this act of learning – becoming an effective listener – is not an optional extra. To listen effectively you'll have to be able to grasp and understand what is said to you; you'll have to be able to recognize the rhythms and patterns present in those streams of words; you'll have to be able to discriminate between fact and opinion, logic and emotion, bias and prejudice. But it isn't just the words that will be important, you'll have to be able to listen to the spaces between those words and the gestures, postures and facial expressions that accompany them. Listening effectively is anything but a passive role.

# Effective listening skills

The skills of effective listening are proactive; they involve you in attending to the speaker, following what she or he says and reflecting that in your responses. Just as gesture, posture and facial expression form an important part of what is said to you, the physical nature of your listening is also important. You'll need to maintain good eye contact with the speaker; you'll need to adopt a 'hearing' posture by leaning slightly forward; you'll need to confirm that you're listening by nodding and by making 'uh huh' or 'hmm' sounds. Your responses should reflect what has been said to you – by paraphrasing its content and asking clarifying questions. And, most important of all, you should maintain your commitment to listening – whatever is said and whatever is your reaction to those words.

All of this means doing things like:

facing the speaker
adopting a posture that is open, i.e. without crossed
arms or legs
leaning towards the speaker
establishing and maintaining good eye contact
being attentively relaxed.

Skilful questioning can also make a considerable contribution to
the listening process. These 'listening' questions should be limited
in number; too many questions disrupt the flow of what the other
side is saying and may leave them feeling that they aren't being
listened to. They should also be the sort of question that is either:

open-ended, or
probing

An open-ended question requires more than a simple 'yes' or 'no'
as an answer as in:

**A:** I'm not happy about the figures you're quoting
**B:** Why is that?

These are the sort of questions that enable the other side to give you
more information. Closed-ended questions rarely do this. When
you use a probing question it should focus the speaker and stop him
or her talking generalities or even rambling. Again, its objective
should be to get the speaker to give you more information. If you
do all of this then not only will you listen effectively, you'll also be
able to respond effectively to what the other side says.

## Conversations and debates

A conversation is actually a quite sophisticated way of
communicating. People who research these things tell us that a
typical conversation involves three or four people and what goes in
it consists of structured 'strings' or sequences of spoken sentences.
The order, content and structure of these sequences are governed
by informal rules; rules about such things as who talks next, how to
interrupt, when it is all right to interrupt, stopping and starting or
how to bring up a new topic. But unlike a lot of our conversations

– that are low key, casual, events – the conversations of your negotiation will have a purpose and, because of that, they will have a cutting edge. As such they'll take you beyond the boundaries of ordinary conversation. They'll involve debate, with cases argued for and against; they'll aim to ventilate a question or a subject, to establish a point or even to elicit truth. The subject of these discussions is, of course, the shape, form and content of a potential agreement and this is deliberated over from your and the other side's viewpoints until a conclusion or endpoint is reached.

Be assured that what goes on in these discussions is crucial to your negotiation. For in them is contained the shared struggle to find agreement – one that you'll both accept and support. Because of this, it is easy for these discussions or dialogues to become heated; allegations and counter-allegations may be made, even tempers lost. It is important to try and stop this happening and to use your assertion skills if it starts to happen. You must – if you're going to succeed – keep calm. You must, as you saw in Chapter 7, use the Three S's of Cool Negotiation:

- Spot what's happening
- Step away from the anger
- Speak assertively.

Don't react to what you hear as insults or abuse – stay calm and stay in control. Remember deals aren't won, they're *made* and that 'making' will take place during these discussions. These are the conversations that make a difference to the success – or failure – of your negotiation. In these you interact with people; your understanding of them or the subject that you're discussing will change. If your negotiation is going to be successful then the conversations that follow your or the other side's proposals should, in the end, take you into the negotiating space that, as you saw in Chapter 2, is called the Bargaining Zone.

## What next?

In the next chapter you will explore the space in your negotiation where agreements are made or lost – the Bargaining Zone.

# Checklist ✔

In this chapter you have seen that:

        it is best to open your negotiation by being:

           – pleasant ☐

           – firm ☐

           – assertive. ☐

       you and the other side will, at least, share:

          – a desire to reach an agreement ☐

          – a wish to do that as pleasantly as possible. ☐

      your opening proposal can be suggestions about the agenda of your negotiation. ☐

      this agenda will give you the bridge you need to move to your first agreement. ☐

      when you make your opening proposal make sure that you:

         – leave room for manoeuvre ☐

         – indicate any conditions attached to it ☐

         – seek their reactions to it ☐

         – don't make any:

            • concessions ☐

            • exclusions ☐

            • unrealistic or extreme offers. ☐

     it is important to respond to the other side's proposal carefully, asking for further information or more time if you need them. ☐

     it is vital to listen effectively. ☐

     when you ask questions make sure that they're:

        – open ☐

       or

        – probing. ☐

■ make sure you discuss proposals in ways that are:
  – cool ☐
  – calm ☐
  – constructive ☐
  – effective. ☐

# 9 | THE BARGAINING ZONE

*Bargains made in speed are commonly repented at leisure.*

**George Pettie**

People bargain everywhere – in market places, on street corners, in board rooms, offices, kitchens, restaurants and bedrooms. They bargain on the plains of Africa, in the snows of Alaska, the jungles of Asia and the deserts of Arabia. In all of these places and in many, many more – you'll find people bargaining. When they do so what they're trying to do is to find a way of agreeing about an act of exchange. This bargaining is about haggling, wrangling, dealing or bartering – and it also lies at the core of your negotiation.

But bargaining doesn't stand on its own. Its roots lie deep in your preparation, it is ushered in by the 'Hellos', 'Good mornings' and handshakes of your openings, you enter it through the doorways of your and the other side's proposals. In it you'll find the heart of your struggle to reach agreement – an agreement that both you and the other side will accept and support. Doing this – and doing it well – is obviously important. It will demand much of you as a negotiator. You'll need to be able to use your negotiating skills and use them in ways that are consistent and credible.

In the remaining chapters of Part Two you'll look at how you can achieve that. First, in this chapter, you'll look at the shape and detail of the area in which all this bargaining takes place – the Bargaining Zone. Then, in Chapter 10, you'll look at 'tricks of the trade' that successful negotiators – those with a track record of success in negotiation and implementation – use to navigate this zone.

# The Bargaining Zone

You'll cross the outer boundaries of the Bargaining Zone when you:

- make your first proposal, or
- respond – with a counter-proposal – to the other side's first proposal.

If you're negotiating over the price of your new car, your opening offer will be a low one and the other side – the car dealer – will have responded by naming a price that's high. Remember that, as you saw in the last chapter, you'll need to make this opening offer in a way that's clear, brief and confident and that tells the dealer about your desire to reach an agreement. This, your first offer, must:

- leave you room for manoeuvre
- NOT contain any concessions or exclusions.

Remember, this is your *opening* offer. But if you're going to use it as a springboard to success, then it shouldn't be one that's unrealistic or extreme. Your earlier efforts at preparation and research should help you to make sure that that doesn't happen. Nor should it be one that's hedged about with multiple conditions and qualifications – the time for those is later.

The gap between this opening offer of yours and the other side's counter-offer may, at first, seem enormous – even unbridgeable. But don't worry, all's not lost. Remember – car dealers need to sell cars and you need to buy a car. This is why you're here, this is the common ground between you and the dealer. The territory that these offers open up for you is called the Bargaining Zone.

When you take a look at the contours and dimensions of this zone in Figure 9.1, what you'll see is that its boundaries are marked by your (the buyer) and the car dealer's (the seller's) opening offers. But what you'll also see inside the zone are:
The Buyer's:

- Ideal Offer
- Realistic Offer
- Highest Offer

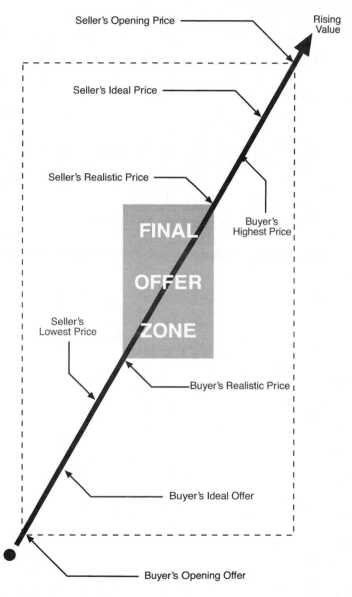

**Figure 9.1 The Bargaining Zone**

and the Seller's:

■ Ideal Price
■ Realistic Price
■ Lowest Price.

Take time to study Figure 9.1, look at the relative levels of these offers and prices. You'll also be able to see that:

■ the Seller's Opening Price is considerably more than the Buyer's Opening Offer.
■ the Seller's Ideal Price is quite a lot more than the Buyer's Ideal Offer.
■ the Seller's Realistic Price is closer to but still more than the Buyer's Realistic Offer.

All of these seem to underline the differences between you and the seller with the seller's prices being consistently higher than your (the buyer's) offer values. But when you look at the figures for the highest and lowest values you'll find a difference. For you'll find that:

■ the Buyer's Highest Offer exceeds the Seller's Lowest Price.

This overlap – where the buyer's highest 'might-do' figure is higher than the seller's 'won't go below' price – is important. For without it there's no space for you and the seller to negotiate in. You can see this overlap more clearly when you take a look at Figure 9.2.

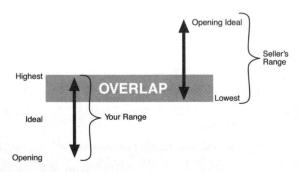

**Figure 9.2  The price and offer overlap**

During your preparation you focused in on the absolute level of the values that make up your range. You decided that, for example, while you were prepared to pay up to $12,100 for your car, that your ideal price would be $10,000 and that you thought a realistic price would probably be $11,300. Now, in the Bargaining Zone, the emphasis is different. For here, it is the relative values – the differences between your offers and the car dealer's prices – that are important. Let's look at this in more detail. The car dealer will have – just as you do – a range of values. When we compare these to your values what we see is:

|  | You | Car Dealer | Difference (yours–dealer's) |
|---|---|---|---|
| Ideal | $11,000 | $13,000 | – $2,000 |
| Realistic | $11,300 | $12,500 | – $1,200 |
| Lowest or Highest | $12,100 | $12,000 | + $100 |

What you can see here is interesting. For you can see that the differences between your and the dealer's values decrease as you move from Ideal to Highest (or Lowest) and you can see that they change in relative value. When you compare Ideal values you can see that the car dealer's is more than yours – but when you compare the highest and lowest, yours is larger than the dealer's. This is the all-important overlap that, as you saw earlier, you need if you're going to complete your negotiation.

## The Overlap

Using this overlap is an important part of what you'll do in the Bargaining Zone. For if there isn't an overlap then there'll be a gap, and a gap – with the other side's lowest price being higher than your highest offer – means that your and the other side's chosen value ranges have no ground to bargain in. In short, a situation that presents little hope of success.

Now you can begin to see and appreciate the importance and value of your preparation. For it is in that preparation that you identify and create the overlap between the value ranges. Without thorough, effective preparation, this overlap and your chance of success would be at the mercy of the fickle hand of fate – having an overlap would be a random chance event. You can also make a major contribution to the creation or reinforcement of this overlap when, as you saw in the last chapter, you search at the beginning of your negotiation for common ground between you and the other side.

But what happens if you don't have an overlap? Is that it? Do you pack up and go home? The answer to these questions is in two parts. Firstly, and I'm going to say it again – even if you don't like it – you *shouldn't* have a gap. If you've done your research properly, if – as you saw in Chapter 2 – you've walked, looked and shopped – then you should have got some idea about whether a deal is possible and even what sort of a deal that might be. You'll have taken notes – to remind you and the salesperson of what was said – and you'll have read through the car magazines to find out what sort of discounts are usual and what sort of part exchange values are possible. All of this should not only enable you to pitch all of your offer values at pragmatic and realistic levels, it should also give you an overlap.

But if it doesn't, if you find yourself facing a yawning gap, then what *do* you do? The answer depends on why the gap is there. For example, if you are facing a gap and you're confident that your research has been done properly and your value range is realistic, then the chances are that you're facing someone who is:

■ either confused or hasn't done their research properly
■ or is going for a win–lose rather than a win–win outcome.

Someone who is confused or ill-prepared is generally easier to deal with than someone who is hell bent on 'beating' you. You can get rid of the confusion and increase their understanding by sharing your information with them – assuming, that is, that it is not confidential information. The way that you do this is important. Nobody likes to be told that they're wrong; none of us likes to have our noses rubbed in our mistakes. So go easy and share what you know gently. They may even need a break to read and digest the information that you're sharing with them. If, however, you find that this approach doesn't generate a constructive response, then you need to face the reality that you're dealing with an aggressive 'win–lose' negotiator. 'Win–lose' negotiators are like sharks. They need to keep moving, all the time, and they're also messy feeders. So don't over-expose yourself, but be assertive and handle his or her threats, insults, intimidation, bluff and bluster in the ways that were identified in Chapter 4. In the end, if the message doesn't get through to them, break off the negotiation and take your business elsewhere.

If, however, the gap is one that you've created, then what do you do? This can happen for a number of reasons. For example, it can happen because you've allowed yourself to be rushed into a negotiation before you're ready – as when the salesperson tells you 'it's a special price and will be gone next week', or when your boss gets pushy for results. It can also happen because you're not being flexible enough, you've allowed yourself to get stuck with a particular way of looking at things. If you've done your research properly, then this shouldn't happen because in doing that you'll have identified and reviewed all of the potential or alternative strategies for you to reach your outcome. So if the one you're using isn't going to work, then throw it away and use one of the others. Doing this can take nerve and courage. It is often better launched after an adjournment or a break so that the other side can accept it as a real shift in direction or pace, as indeed it may well be. You may also find yourself facing a gap when you lose sight of your value range or your goals. This can easily happen in long and complex negotiations or in fast-paced negotiations in which the offers and counter-offers fly thick and fast. You can avoid this happening if you go into the negotiating space with key points written down on a piece of paper so you can read – almost at a glance – what your value range and goals are. But don't let the other side see it!

## Moving up and on

Fortunately, most – though not all – of your negotiations will have an overlap and will find their way eventually through to an agreement of one sort or another. But having an overlap is still a long way from having an agreement. What you need to do now is to move on up – from exploring and sounding out – into talking about and acting on specific proposals.

The ways and means that you'll use to move your negotiation along are called, as you saw in Chapter 4, tactics. In that chapter you saw a number of examples of the general tactics that you can use to move your negotiation. You also saw that any tactic you use must be complementary to or compatible with your strategy for that negotiation. Now, you can look at the tactics that you can use to move your negotiation from the general to the specific, from the explored to the proposed and from the proposed to the agreed. The point of these tactics is to move you and the other side closer together, to find ways of increasing the opportunities for agreement and which one you use must be a matter for your own judgement.

| TACTIC | COMMENTARY |
|---|---|
| Fragmenting | When you use this tactic you literally fragment the problem that's blocking the way forward down into smaller, more manageable, and soluble issues. Its cost might be that you lose momentum; its gain, that you start to agree things. |
| Variables and options | You should never give up the search for new variables or new options. If the price is right even the most concrete of features or the most intractable of deadlines can suddenly become negotiable. |
| What if ...? | The 'What if ...?' or the 'Supposing I ...' question or suggestion is a very powerful way of opening up new avenues of discussion. Don't over-use though, or you'll leave the impression that you're not sure what you do want. |
| By-passing | When deadlock looms it can often be useful to temporarily put aside an apparently intractable issue. Only do this when you sense that staying with the issue is becoming potentially damaging to the chance of agreement. You must return to it |

| TACTIC (continued) | COMMENTARY (continued) |
|---|---|
| | – even if it is only to jointly acknowledge that it has now been overtaken by events. |
| Willingness | Saying that you're 'willing to consider' the other side's proposal or that you're 'willing to acknowledge the strength of their argument ' can – without any commitment from you – begin to create an atmosphere of trust and understanding. You need these to build an agreement. |
| Concession and trade | You must never concede something without gaining something in trade in return. Concessions must *always* be made grudgingly and reluctantly and shouldn't be made too early. |
| Hard work and commitment | This is a bit of a 'double-edged sword' and should be used with care. The harder and longer you work together, the more committed the other side become to finding an agreement, and the more committed they are, the more likely they are to compromise – rather than go back to square one. Take care though – for this also applies to you as well! |
| Periodic summaries | Periodic summaries or taking time out to review the progress made so far can be a powerful aid to movement forward. Such a review underlines the progress that's been made and builds a firm foundation for further progress. It can also, however, reveal differences in understanding about the current position, differences that need to be resolved before you can move on. Doing this early in your negotiation is a far, far better alternative than struggling with it at the end. |
| Saving face | The face you're saving when you use this tactic is the other side's. Losing face – by backing down or 'giving in' – can be very |

| TACTIC (continued) | COMMENTARY (continued) |
|---|---|
| | difficult to do. When it looks as if this is going to happen your job is not to gloat – it's to help. You can do this by:<br>– identifying the benefits to them<br>– minimizing the benefits to you<br>– praising their wisdom and courage<br>– avoiding any win–lose comments. |
| Decision signals | We all send signals when we're approaching a decision. These can be a change in the way we speak: from tentative to firm and confident or from discursive statements to crisp and short ones, or actions like gathering together our papers. When you see these, don't hesitate – act and act quickly. You may need to take a risk but don't worry – risks often lead to the other side making a real commitment. |

Remember, the point of all these tactics is to take you and the other side, together, into the area at the centre of the Bargaining Zone – the Final Offer Zone. What happens in there is what we'll explore in Part Three.

---

**FRIDAY NIGHT**

Getting to this point hadn't been easy. But now – when they were so close to agreement – things had suddenly got 'sticky'. Brett Davies, the plant manager, had almost got the union representative, Janice Long, to agree to her members being paid by credit transfer into their bank accounts instead of cash payment in a wage packet. Brett couldn't work out what the problem was – then he had a brain wave.

'How would it be', he said to Janice, 'if the Accounts Department provided a cheque cashing service – just at Friday lunchtime – for a trial period.' He paused, he could see Janice was interested. 'If that works maybe one of the banks will install an ATM by the gate,' he said.

'Yes,' said Janice, 'then I could still go shopping on a Friday evening.'

## What next?

In the next chapter, you will look at the skills that you will need to gain agreement – the skills of the effective negotiator.

## Checklist ✔

In this chapter you have seen that:

- ■ bargaining is something we all do. ☐
- ■ the act of bargaining lies at the heart of your negotiation. ☐
- ■ you cross the boundaries of the Bargaining Zone when:
  - – you make your first proposal ☐
    or
  - – respond – with a counter-proposal – to the other side's first proposal. ☐
- ■ you saw that the Bargaining Zone contains:

  The Buyer's:
  - – Ideal Offer ☐
  - – Realistic Offer ☐
  - – Highest Offer ☐
- ■ and the Seller's
  - – Ideal Price ☐
  - – Realistic Price ☐
  - – Lowest Price. ☐

■ you also saw that in the Bargaining Zone: ☐
  - the Seller's Opening Price is considerably more than the Buyer's Opening Offer. ☐
  - the Seller's Ideal Price is quite a lot more than the Buyer's Ideal Offer. ☐
  - the Seller's Realistic Price is more than the Buyer's Realistic Offer. ☐

■ in order to reach an agreement there must be an overlap between the other side's and your value range so that the Buyer's Highest Offer is greater than the Seller's Lowest Price. ☐

■ moving your negotiation forward – from general to the specific, or from the explored to the proposed – requires you to choose and use the right tactic. ☐

■ this tactic should move you and the other side closer together, to find ways of increasing the opportunities for agreement. ☐

■ tactics you can use include:
  - fragmenting ☐
  - variables and options ☐
  - what if? ☐
  - by-passing ☐
  - willingness ☐
  - concession and trade ☐
  - hard work and commitment ☐
  - periodic summaries ☐
  - saving face ☐
  - decision signals. ☐

■ the tactic you use must be a matter for your own judgement. ☐

# 10 | NEGOTIATING SKILLS

*A miser and a liar bargain quickly.*

**Proverb**

When the going gets tough in your negotiation you'll need help. 'What do I do next?' you'll be wondering. If you're like most people, the 'this-is-the-way-you-do-it' resource that you'll fall back on is the one that's based on how you did it last time or the time before – your experience. This shouldn't really surprise you – for, as the proverb says, 'Experience is the father of wisdom'. Building up this log book of experience starts early. As very young children, you and I learnt that our cries could lead to our needs being answered. But as we grew older that particular negotiating ploy worked less effectively and we had to learn other ways. And so, we looked, watched and listened – even marvelled – at the ways that the adults and older children around us used to get their needs answered, to navigate their way through the inevitable conflicts of family life. You and I took these, our first lessons in negotiation, literally at our mother's knee. This learning process still continues – although not at our mother's knee – and you and I will go on – as long as we live, expanding and refining the arts and crafts of our negotiation.

But is all of this enough – and if it is, why aren't we all brilliant negotiators? The answer has three parts to it:

■ firstly, we haven't all had the same sort of exposure to either the act of negotiating or skilful negotiating

■ secondly, our abilities to learn from our experiences differ

■ and finally, many of the attempts to establish 'best practice' patterns for negotiating use laboratory simulations rather than real negotiations.

Nevertheless, there is enough negotiating wisdom about to provide you with some clear indications as to how a skilled and effective negotiator behaves during the process of negotiation.

## Effective or defective

But before you probe into this wisdom, you have a decision to take. You have to decide how you're going to measure or assess the results of your negotiation. One of the easiest and quickest ways of doing this is to look at what the words 'efficient' and 'effective' mean – first in general terms, then when you use them to describe a negotiator. Being effective is often confused with being efficient. But the two are actually quite different. Efficiency is about resource usage – as in miles per gallon for a car or $ cost per square metre of floor area for a new building. Effectiveness brings in another dimension. You'll say that something is effective when it gets results – where and when you want them. Being effective may, or may not, mean that you are efficient. Being effective means that the desired outcome is generated at the right place and at the right time. But efficiency and effectiveness aren't all that you need to consider; there's also adaptability. An adaptable negotiator is one who is able to change or modify the way that she or he negotiates to meet the challenges and demands of a varying negotiating situation. From all of this you can see that an effective negotiator:

■ gets results
■ gets results where and when they are needed, and
■ does so by being, amongst other things, adaptable.

## Ways and means

So how does she or he achieve all of the above three points? Views differ about this. From one point of view, it is down to your personality, the way you are as a person. From another point of view, it is the skills you have and how you use them. From yet another, it is all down to a bunch of ways of doing things or micro-behaviours. Let's take a look at each of these in turn.

## Personality traits

It is perhaps not surprising that the list of qualities, characteristics or traits that an effective negotiator's personality is supposed to have is not only long; it is also one that's attracted great comment. Many of these comments have much in common with the sort of leadership theory that tells us that leaders are born, not made – a theory that has little research evidence to support it. The level of confusion rises further when you look at the labels given to the sorts of behaviours that effective negotiators show; labels that are generalized and diffuse. Lists of these include: being empathic, fair, patient and flexible; showing respect, responsibility and self-discipline; and having integrity, stamina and a sense of humour. Some of these – like flexibility, a sense of humour and stamina – are characteristics that you'll readily recognize as being desirable. But others – such as showing respect – are too generalized or less acceptable – as in self-discipline – or less connected to the real world of our negotiations – such as being 'fair'. But that's not to say that you should throw these out or even reject the idea they can be used to define an effective negotiator. Far from it, but do ask yourself how many good negotiators that you know, actively and regularly show *all* these traits. If, like me, you come up with a list of none, then perhaps we should seriously consider adding 'walks on water' to the list.

## Skills

The *Oxford English Dictionary* tells us that when we have a skill we are 'capable of accomplishing something with precision and certainty' and that we have 'practical knowledge in combination with ability'. If you're going to be an effective negotiator, then you'll certainly need to have ability and expertise and you'll also need to be able to translate those into practical outcomes. But, if we're not going to fall into the trap of being too vague and general in our descriptions, then we need to be more specific and detailed in what we say about the skills of effective negotiation. From all that you've read so far, you should be able to see, for example, that an effective negotiator needs to be able to:

- ■ gather and use knowledge and information about:
    - – the negotiating process
    - – the other side, their past and likely future behaviours
    - – the subject of the negotiation itself
    - – the context of the negotiation.
- ■ analyse information, issues, behaviours, responses, proposals and counter-proposals
- ■ communicate effectively
- ■ develop and use her or his social skills to effect
- ■ generate and maintain positive attitudes towards:
    - – the other side
    - – the negotiating process's likely outcome.

For almost all of us the skills on this list aren't inaccessible or even difficult. After all, if you can run your own business, manage a team or run a busy household, you've almost certainly been using them – even if you didn't realize it. However, the difficulty for some of us will lie either in the breadth or the particular application focus of this skill bundle. But before you give up, before you throw your hands in the air shouting 'I'll never be an effective negotiator!', remember that being a negotiator isn't new for you. You've actually been a negotiator all of your life and in doing that you've developed many of these skills. What you need to do now is to look at the how and when of refining and adding to those skills. One of the easiest ways of doing that appears when you look at the things that effective negotiators do – and don't do – in negotiations.

## Ways of doing things

Most of the examples that follow are based on observed behaviours or, to put it another way, the things that skilled and experienced negotiators have been seen to do to get results. But as you read it try to remember that this isn't a treatise on negotiating by numbers –

you don't have to do it *exactly* this way. Try and pick out the principles involved and use them to find your own way of doing it.

The behaviours observed fell into two broad groups:

■ those that were used *less often* by skilled negotiators and more often by less skilled or average negotiators.

■ those that were used *more often* by skilled negotiators and less often by less skilled or average negotiators.

These we'll call the 'Don'ts' and 'Do's' of skilled negotiating.

## Don'ts

Skilled negotiators are good communicators – they don't use words carelessly. They don't, for example, use words or phrases that might irritate the other side – such as describing their offer as being 'generous' – when it is obvious that it is just one in a series of offers and counter-offers. Other examples of words that irritate are 'fair' or 'reasonable' – particularly when applied to your own offer. These words possess little persuasive power and can often, by implication, leave the other side with the feeling that they are seen as being 'unfair' or 'unreasonable'. While there are few negotiators who would use insults or judgemental phrases or words, it appears to be quite common for average negotiators – but rare for skilled negotiators – to indulge in the use of uncalled for and self-flattering words and phrases. Examples would be 'our generous offer' or 'we've waited patiently for your response'.

Another 'Don't' lies in the speed and frequency with which negotiators respond to each other's proposals. 'Knee jerk' responses and counter-proposals are often seen to indicate disagreement or to be 'blocking' whereas lower frequency or delayed responses and counter-proposals are seen to be more thoughtful and considered. You've already seen how important it is to avoid becoming heated and emotional during your negotiation. When this happens, both you and the other side can easily get drawn into an ascending spiral of attack and counter-attack. Skilled negotiators don't do this. But it is, in the course of events, often necessary to attack. When skilled negotiators do this they often give little or no warning – unlike average negotiators who tend to give early warnings, rising up the attack/counter-attack spiral slowly at first but then accelerating as they rise. These less-skilled or average negotiators are also seen to 'over-egg the pudding' when it comes to the use of reasons in support of the argument or case they are making. Skilled negotiators use far fewer arguments but choose those that they do use with care. This not only avoids confusion and dispute, it also recognizes that, in the end, your case is only as strong as its weakest support argument.

A final example of the things that skilled negotiators don't do lies in the ways that they use to flag up their disagreement. Most of us would see it to be entirely logical to first state that we disagree and then follow this with an explanation of why we disagree. Skilled negotiators reverse this order, giving first their reasons or explanations and then, second, the statement of disagreement. On page 113 there are some examples of these 'don'ts'.

## Do's

In addition to all the things that we've seen that they don't do, skilled negotiators also emphasize certain sorts of behaviour during their negotiations. For example, they tend to give prior notice of what they're going to do. When asking a question they'll preface it with 'May I ask a question?', or when they're about to make a suggestion they'll start by saying 'If I may make a suggestion ...'. When you do this it focuses the listener's attention on the action that's to follow as well as introducing a space in proceedings – which gives the listener time to 'shift gear'. But as we saw earlier, this 'I'm-going-to-do-this-next' sort of labelling isn't used with disagreeing.

The skilled negotiator will also summarize and test a lot – as in 'Let me check where I think we've got to'. Doing this reduces the chances of misunderstandings occurring and also encourages clear communication. Alongside these, the experienced negotiator will also:

■ reflect what she or he thinks has been said as in:
   'So do I understand that you're saying you can't agree to our proposal.'

## DON'TS OF SKILLED NEGOTIATION

### Irritators

**Management Negotiator:** I believe that we are making an offer which, given the current state of the market, is not just fair but also downright generous.

### Over-responsive Counter-proposals

**Negotiator A:** I suggest that we have a coffee before we drive over to John's.

**Negotiator B:** How about having coffee when we get there?

### Defence/Attack Patterns

**Negotiator A:** What you are asking is ridiculous. If you had any understanding of basic economics you would know what I'm talking about.

**Negotiator B:** If you had any understanding of people then you wouldn't be proposing such an arrangement.

**Negotiator A:** In all of my 20 years as a manager I've never met such an uncooperative attitude as yours.

**Negotiator B:** I don't care about your 20 years experience, *etc. etc. etc.*

### Dilution by Argument

**Management Negotiator:** I believe that this proposal for revised working hours is the right proposal because it enables the company to be more responsive to its customers, make better use of the part-time female workers and solves our car parking problems.

**Union Negotiator:** It's funny that you should mention the car parking – I've had it in mind to talk to you about that for some time.

### Signalling Disagreement

**Negotiator:** I disagree with your proposals because they don't go far enough to meet my needs and will cost me too much to implement.

■ ask open-ended and probing questions in order to get more information as in:

'Can you explain that in more detail?'

■ express concern about implementation as in:

'I'm concerned about how this is all going to work.'

Many of these are used to exert control of what's going on in the negotiation as well as providing thinking time while the other side is occupied in generating an answer or response.

Skilled negotiators are also much more open about their feelings than average negotiators are. For example, they'll say things like:

'I'm beginning to feel some concern about whether we're going to reach an agreement today.'

or

'I'm uncertain about whether my members will accept that.'

Doing this often builds higher levels of trust in the developing relationship that she or he has with the other side. This trust, together with confidence in other's continued co-operation and a joint determination to avoid rows and arguments, are all present in the behaviour of skilled negotiators.

Below are some examples of the 'Do's' of skilled negotiating behaviour.

---

**DO'S OF SKILLED NEGOTIATION**
**Signalling**

**Negotiator:**  I wonder if I might ask a question – how many times has this happened?

**Testing and Summarizing**

**Negotiator:**  If I can summarize where I think we've got to – you have said that you will be able to accept our revised proposals about pay structures but have difficulty with the current working hours proposals. Have I understood you correctly?

---

**Implementation Concern**

**Negotiator:**   I would like to ask some more questions about the new duty rota and how it will work, since in the end my members will have to work this new rota.

**Seeking Information**

**Negotiator:**   At what size of order would I get a bigger discount?

**Statements about Feelings**

**Negotiator:**   We've been talking now for almost an hour and I'm beginning to feel some concern about the big differences that there still are between us.

# What next?

Now you should be ready to move on to Part Three. In this you will look at how a negotiation is brought to a close, how breakdowns are handled and how the outcomes agreed are successfully implemented.

# Checklist ☑

In this chapter you have seen that:

- ■ most of us draw on our experience to tell us what to do in a negotiation.                                                                    ☐
- ■ good negotiators:
    - – get results                                                                                            ☐
    - – gets results where and when they are needed   ☐
    - – do so by being, amongst other things, adaptable.                                                                          ☐
- ■ effective negotiators behave in ways that:
    - – use words carefully                                                                    ☐
    - – give notice of what they're about to do               ☐
    - – give reasons first, then conclusions                   ☐
    - – use summaries and testing a lot                           ☐

  – use open-ended and probing questions                ☐
  – express their feelings, but do so coolly.            ☐
■ effective negotiators don't:
  – use words carelessly or to irritate                 ☐
  – use 'knee-jerk' responses                           ☐
  – get drawn into attacks and counter-attacks          ☐
  – dilute arguments                                    ☐
  – give conclusions first, then reasons.               ☐

*Part Three*

# COMPLETING
# YOUR NEGOTIATION

*The unfinished is nothing.*
Henri Frederic Amiel

# 11 | AGREEING AND CLOSING

*It is better to lose the saddle than the horse.*

**Italian proverb**

At the beginning of this book – way back in Chapter 1 – you saw a definition. It told you that negotiation is the way that people identify mutually acceptable decisions and agree the what and how of future actions. Since then, you've seen what's needed to get to these 'mutually acceptable decisions'. In Part One you looked at the preparation needed, the ways and means of setting your objectives, the finding out about the other side, the choices you need to make about the strategies and tactics you are to follow, the where, how and when of your negotiation and the communication and social skills you need to complete it. More recently, in Part Two, you looked at the nitty-gritty of your negotiation: the ways and means of your opening, talking, listening and proposing, the Bargaining Zone and the negotiating skills you need.

Now, in Part Three, you'll look at how you can complete your negotiation, how its agreements can be converted from words to actions and then implemented. But not all of your negotiations will flow easily from beginning to end. Some will stall, become deadlocked, teeter towards breakdown and in this section you'll also look at how you can respond to these situations.

## Agreements

To say that the agreement that your negotiation creates is important seems almost unnecessary. Since the start of your preparation it has been the desired outcome of your negotiation; it lay at the heart of the first step you took – that of deciding what it was that you wanted to achieve. Now, as we approach the end of your negotiation, this agreed outcome is closer than it ever was before.

But agreements can be fickle creatures and are often subject to the vagaries of human nature. As the nineteenth-century German statesman, Otto von Bismarck, told us: 'When you say that you agree to a thing in principle, you mean that you have not the slightest intention of carrying it out in practice.' Even when there is no intention to deceive, your agreement will still have to avoid the pitfalls of misunderstanding, forgetfulness and changeable minds before it can reach the gateway that leads to its full and real completion. Avoiding all of these is essential. But, before we see how to do that, let's first look at how you can make that key jump – from decision to agreement – and make it without falling.

## The Final Offer Zone

In Chapter 9 you entered the Bargaining Zone. By the end of the chapter – after a sequence of offer and counter-offer – you reached the edge of another crucial area. For there, at the heart of the Bargaining Zone, is the area in which your agreement will be forged – the Final Offer Zone. If you look back at the diagram of the Bargaining Zone (page 97), you'll see that the boundaries of this, the Final Offer Zone, lie at values identified early in your and the other side's preparation – those of your and their 'realistic' values. In the early days of your preparation you arrived at this 'realistic' value because it was the price or offer that your experience and research told you that you'd probably finish up paying.

Moving on and up from this view of what is realistic isn't an easy task. After all, you arrived here because of your research; you'd surveyed the market, you'd found out all about the usual discounts and part-exchange values and you'd ferreted out what other people are getting or paying. But this is the point for courage – not caution – and if you want to reach an agreement then you must be prepared to move. But, before you make your mind up on this, it is worth reviewing your value range. Check it out, make sure that it's current – after all, prices and values do move, sometimes quite suddenly. When you're doing that it is also a good time to stand back and look at where you've got to. See if you can see any areas where you haven't got what you wanted. Try and find something that can be changed – even at this late hour – and see if doing that will restore the balance in your favour; try and find some way that this change can be linked to some compromise that the other side is asking you to make. When you've done all of this you'll probably find that you've got a subtly – but significantly – different view of your negotiation. You'll be able to see just how thorough your preparation was, how much you've actually achieved and how close you are to agreement. You may also have identified further possible shifts or changes. At this point it is also worth remembering that, in the end, value is in the eye of the beholder. It is the value that your outcome has for *you* that counts – rather than what someone else feels about it or what the Green or Black or Red book says. When you've done all that then you're ready to move forward.

# Agreeing

Reaching an agreement with someone is rarely a straightforward or an easy task. The pathway to that final handshake that is often taken – between men, at least – to symbolize a deal or an agreement, is often littered with pitfalls or booby-traps. Getting to an agreement requires patience, skill and ability. But it is not something that you do on your own – as the proverb tells us 'it takes two to make a bargain'. So what are the ways and means by which you generate an agreement?

This first step towards achieving that agreement is an obvious one: it is that of avoiding, dodging around, side-stepping the word 'NO'. Many of the things that you do in the early stages of the negotiation are designed to avoid that NO. Your strategy was created with the purpose of reaching agreement – rather than *dis*-agreement – and the tactics that you used were aimed towards that endpoint. Your opening proposal was deliberately designed to leave room for manoeuvre, to seek reactions and leave aside any exclusions. All of these and other of your actions have been focused towards the endpoint that you're now approaching – that of making an agreement. But, as someone, somewhere, once said, 'there's many a slip 'twixt cup and lip'. If you want to maximize your chances of reaching that endpoint then here are some of the actions that you can take to help yourself:

| ACTION | OBJECTIVE |
|---|---|
| **Summarize** | Summaries are almost always good. In Chapter 9 you saw how they provide a firm foundation for further movement, how they remind you and the other side about how much progress you've made. Now, at this point in your negotiation, their purpose is different; it's to check out if you're ready for the final two actions: agreeing and closing. But you must make sure your summary covers all the points you've discussed. |
| **Revisiting early issues** | Earlier in your negotiation you may have decided to by-pass a difficult issue. This was probably done in the hope that making progress in other areas may make it easier to revisit at a later time. Now is the last of those later times. But this revisiting will only work if:<br><br>■ you've genuinely made progress since then, and<br><br>■ there's a greater degree of trust between you and the other side.<br><br>If neither of these are there, then you're probably not ready yet. If they are, then make sure that you resolve these issues – now. |
| **Concessions** | Making or accepting a concession can, at the right time, shift your negotiation from deadlock to delight. But take care – for giving away or accepting something that you'd clung on to or rejected earlier in the negotiation can be seen as an act of illogicality – or weakness. It's still worth stressing that in making the concession you're also making a trade – and make sure that you are. |

| | |
|---|---|
| **Splitting it down the middle** | One of the ways that you can use to shift out of a sticky patch is to propose a solution that sits mid-way between the previous opposing proposals. For this to work you really do have to 'split the difference' – equally and fairly. You'll need to make sure that neither you nor the other side is seen to be gaining at the expense of the other or losing to the benefit of the other. |
| **This or that** | Another way to regain traction – and move on – is to present two equal, but different, alternative proposals. Doing it indicates your willingness to reach an agreement. But the down side of doing it is the risk that you lose credibility – remember you'd said that your last offer was your final offer. There's no guarantee that the other side will accept either offer. |
| **The whole package** | This is the bit about the whole being greater than the sum of its parts – or, at least, that's the way it seems. Sewing together or relating the separate parts of your agreement can bring up a 'gloss' on your potential agreement that wasn't seen before. It can also reveal synergistic benefits that you'd missed earlier when you were involved in the detail. Either – or both – of these can provide that extra push that'll take you both into agreement. |
| **New ideas or proposals** | It's argued that introducing new proposals shifts the balance, destabilizes the stand-off. But ringing in the new at this point in your negotiation can also undo all your earlier good work. You can easily be seen as being manipulative or time-wasting – and if this happens it's back-to-the-drawing-board time. |

# Timing

The second step towards achieving an agreement is that of getting your timing right.The when of your agreement is just as crucial as its how. Get it wrong and your hoped-for agreement will fall to earth. Get it right and your agreement – and you – will do a 'victory roll'. Having said that, picking the 'right' time isn't an easy task. For that reason most people delay and leave reaching this agreement for far too long. What happens then is that the other side misreads or misunderstands your delay – they think that you're unenthusiastic or disinterested – and they don't understand why. 'We'd been getting along so well' th∘v say to themselves. As a result they may become confused or defensive. What happens then is that what was, up to that point, a well-prepared and well-conducted negotiation begins a slide towards failure.

Choosing the 'right' time is partly instinct and partly common sense. When someone is ready to agree, they tell you. It'll be writ large in the way they sit forward, the way they look at you, the way that they speak. All you've got to do is to train yourself to look for the signs. But that's not all that you can do – you can also ensure that you'll get the time right by keeping the idea of closure to the front of your mind right from the very beginning of your negotiation. When you're looking for it as early and as keenly as this then two things will happen:

    **1** The other side will see that you're ready to close – even perhaps before you realize it, and

    **2** You'll recognize the 'right time' because it arrives at the same time as:

- an agreement that's acceptable to both you and the other side
- ticks against all or most of the items on your objectives checklist
- the fact that time's running out, the shop's about to shut etc.

When this happens you need to switch into closure mode.

# Closing

The act of closing your negotiation, or closure, means – according to the *Oxford English Dictionary* – 'an agreeing upon terms, a coming to an arrangement with'. When you and the other side reach the point at which the 'mutual acceptability' of your individual decisions has become so obvious that it can't be ignored – then it's time for closure. But closure doesn't happen spontaneously and you'll still have some things to do in order to trigger it.

The first of these is to prepare yourself. What you're about to do is important. It is the outcome of all the hard work that you've put in; it is the climax of a sequence of well-prepared and planned activities. All of this will create a set of mixed feelings for you. You'll probably, on the one hand, be feeling nervous – 'What if I get it wrong?' you'll be thinking. You may also be feeling rather reluctant to see it finish, a bit sad that it's all coming to an end and at the same time you may be feeling unsure as to whether the deal on the table is the best that you can get. When all of this happens, take a break. In that break just go back over it all. Remind yourself of your objectives, compare them with what's before you now. If they're different, ask yourself if you can accept the differences and why they've come about? If you can't – then you're really not ready to close and there's more negotiating to be done. But if you can – then what's next is that you'll go over the way that you're going to present your final offer. You'll do this with yourself or your partner or with your team. You'll pick out and underline the advantages of this final offer, you'll decide how you're going to present it and you'll get yourself in a positive and up-beat frame of mind.

The next thing to do is obvious – it's that you get back out there and make that offer – and do it well.

# Making the offer

Doing this well isn't as easy as it might seem. It takes care, thought and preparation to do it well. For example, you need to use all of your skills to generate the right atmosphere – one that's calm, constructive and positive. You need to reinforce the fact that this *is* your final offer. You can do that by speaking clearly with an up-beat, confident, tone and by using short crisp sentences – rather then the less formal, digressive and open-ended ones you've used earlier in the negotiation. It often helps if you introduce this offer by reflecting, briefly, upon the hard work that both sides have put in. You may also choose to praise the other side, thanking them for their hard work, patience and understanding. This final offer might be one that you'll either make or confirm in writing – in contrast to the verbal offers you've made before. All of these and other actions that you take should be aimed at emphasizing the importance of what you're doing. When you've done it – made the final offer – you should use your body language to underline its finality. Make a move towards packing your papers away, look as if you're going to leave – rather than sitting back and waiting for an expected response, as you did earlier in the negotiation. If this seems a take-it-or-leave-it sort of attitude, it isn't; it is designed to make it clear to the other side that, as far as you're concerned, the discussions have gone as far as they can. You may even want to make that clear by saying such things as 'I've no more room for further movement' or 'I have already made more concessions than I intended to'. Once they've heard your final offer the other side may need a brief recess to discuss it. Recess or no, if you've got it right, then they'll come back just as clearly – with one of two replies – 'Yes' or 'No'. If you've got it wrong, they'll try to twist your arm, fudge the detail or even try a new tack. All of these must be rejected – clearly, firmly and assertively. If the other side is doing this because they're inexperienced, nervous or hesitant, it is all right to be sympathetic – but only up to a point. After all, you've spent a lot of time and effort to get to where you are and they ought to recognize that and be willing to give you a clear and unambiguous 'Yes' or 'No'. If they say 'No' then pack your bags and leave – but without hard feelings or acrimony. After all, you don't know when you'll meet them again. If they say 'Yes', then you need to quickly move to the next step – that of making sure that what you've agreed is written down in black and white.

### CLOSING THE DEAL

Tom could see a deal was close. When he looked across the table he could see interest writ large across Amy's face. 'Have I explained the offer clearly?' he asked. She nodded – but didn't speak. 'Is there anything you don't understand?' he said. She shook her head. He leant forward, slid the paper across the table until its edge touched her arm. 'If you think it's OK, then sign your name at the bottom.' His voice was low and soft. She looked at him. 'OK,' she said. She signed the paper, slowly, seriously, the line under her signature firm and emphatic. That done she turned to look at him again.

'Now,' she said, 'can I have an advance on my allowance 'til Friday?' Tom sighed – 'like father like daughter' he said to himself as he reached for his wallet.

## The written word

Sam Goldwyn, the American film producer, is said to have told us that 'a verbal contract isn't worth the paper it's written on'. When you get to 'Yes' you need to record the deal in writing as soon as you can. This isn't an action that implies uncertainty or a lack of trust. When you think about it you'll realize that it is common sense to record what you've agreed. After all, a written agreement will still be there when the memories of who said what, and when, have faded and gone. In some negotiations the outcome may be important enough for a draft written agreement to be generated there and then – while you and the other side are still together. This can then be signed by both you and the other side. In others, it is sufficient to exchange written drafts at a later date, providing you've a process for handling the differences between these drafts.

Getting this written version of your agreement right is important. When you generate it, you should always bear in mind that it needs to be:

■ brief
■ concise

■ factual
■ accurate.

It isn't a record of who said what and when – it *is* a record of who's involved in the agreement, who gets what, how they get it and when that will occur. It will also record things like how long the agreement will last and what will happen if the agreement is broken by either side. Words like 'fair', 'adequate', 'reasonable', 'significant', 'major' or 'minor' should not appear in your agreement. These are words with diffuse and arguable meanings and there is no place for them in any agreement that's going to work. Once you've got an agreed text for this agreement the next step is get both your and the other side's signatures on it. Until this happens it will have little credibility as an agreement.

# What next?

Not all of your negotiations will flow smoothly to a mutually agreed and satisfactory endpoint. In the next chapter you will explore the how and why of negotiations that get deadlocked, or fail, and examine the ways that you can respond to, and sometimes resolve, these situations.

# Checklist ✔

In this chapter you have seen that:

■ the jump from offer to decision to agreement takes place in the Final Offer Zone.                                                  ☐

■ the boundaries of that zone lie at your and the other side's realistic offer and price values.                               ☐

■ moving from your realistic price into the Final Offer Zone follows your review of your negotiation.                  ☐

■ getting to an agreement takes:

– patience, skill and ability                                                  ☐

– the skilful use of actions such as summarizing, revisiting earlier issues, making concessions, offering to 'split the difference', presenting alternatives or sewing everything together.                        ☐

      – good timing. ☐

■ to close effectively you need to:
- be open to closure from the very beginning of your negotiation ☐
- make it clear that this *is* your final offer ☐
- present your offer in an upbeat and confident manner ☐
- leave the other side some space to review your final offer. ☐

■ if they say 'No' or haggle – move out. ☐

■ if they say 'Yes' – put it in a written form that is:

| | | |
|---|---|---|
| – brief ☐ | – concise ☐ |
| – factual ☐ | – accurate. ☐ |

# 12 | BREAKDOWN AND DEADLOCK

*The test of a man or woman's breeding is how they behave in a quarrel.*

**George Bernard Shaw**

So far, most of what you've looked at has been to do with achieving a good outcome for your negotiation. But, in reality, not all negotiations reach that endpoint. There are – and always will be – negotiations that fail, that fall by the wayside. These are the negotiations that become deadlocked. Their discussions get hung-up on either issues, principles or details, they break down in an explosion of angry words and gestures; tables are banged, doors are slammed. There must be few – if any – of us who haven't experienced these sorts of endings. They come about in our families, our relationships, our jobs and in our market places.

The reasons for this are various. Your own experience of negotiating will tell you that there have been times when you didn't get it right, when you found yourself giving up something that you valued for less than you thought it was worth – and then you 'dug your heels in', refused to budge. This might have happened because you didn't prepare well enough, because your strategy was wrong, because you didn't listen effectively to the other side or because what you wanted to achieve was unrealistic. On other occasions you might have found that you and the other side had both painted yourselves into separate and opposing corners. Your discussions had become frozen. You found yourselves locked into opposing positions that were apparently intransigent and incompatible – and didn't trust each other enough to move.

When these sorts of things happen, you have a choice. You can either :

■ close down the negotiation – and walk away, or

■ you can try to recover the situation.

In this chapter you'll look at the how and why of both of these, together with the ways that you might use to resolve these situations.

# Walking

When you – or I – walk out of a negotiation, we take a risk. That risk is that the other side won't come after us, that they won't call or fax us when things have cooled off, that we lose a chance to reach an agreement with them. For that reason, walking – when you do it – must be a deliberate and considered act. If you walk on impulse or in the heat of the moment, it'll be something that you regret. But if you walk when, after due consideration, you've decided that this negotiation isn't going to get anywhere, then that, as we'll shortly see, is quite a different matter.

To reach the point where you can walk away quietly and calmly, there are several things that you must do:

1 Make space for yourself, space in which you can regain your cool (if you've lost it), a space in which you can think through what's happening and decide the 'if', 'why' and 'when' of your walking. If, when you've done that, you really feel that despite all your preparation and hard work this is the end of the line, then walking is the answer. But this sort of walking isn't an act of despair – it is an act of courage. It takes real courage to admit that your hopes and desires aren't going to be met, and it takes real courage to turn that into an act that's positive.

2 Now you must prepare for the act of walking. Remember this is no act of impulse, it is a calm considered act and it is one that you'll carry out as professionally as you've conducted the rest of your negotiation. So sit down and make some notes to use when you tell the other side:

■ where you are
■ where you see that they are
■ why it won't work.

If you've got time, convert these notes into a letter to give to the other side after you told them, face to face. However you do it, it's important that you don't allocate blame. Just stay with the facts. When you've finished read your letter or your notes through, make sure they say what you want them to, fairly but accurately. Finally, remember to close by thanking them for their time and trouble.

3 Now you're ready to tell them. Doing this face to face is important. It enables you to complement your spoken words with gestures, facial expressions and postures. It also enables you to see their reactions and be able to read their body language. Make sure that you do this in a way that's courteous and considered, and always, always, leave a window open for future communication.

4 When you've finished saying what you want to say – go. Don't look back, don't hesitate – just go.

If the boot's on the other foot – and someone walks out on you – then you've got a different and more difficult choice to make. For you can stop them, or let them go. Which you do depends on whether their going is driven by frustration, impulse or anger or whether it is, like yours above, a considered act. If they are acting out of anger or impulse then you should probably let them go, but do make sure that you get in touch with them later when the anger or impulse has had time to subside. When you do that, don't open your conversation with a judgement on their walking out, offer them the chance to start again. If their walking out seems to you to be a purposeful and considered act or staged for effect, it is worth trying to stop them going – but don't lose face or position by doing so. If you fail to stop them, make sure that you've left a communication window open for the future. There will, of course, be exceptions to both of the above. There will be upset, even angry, walk-outs where your instincts tell you to delay the other side, and there will be considered, but staged, walk-outs where you'll be happy to see them go. Listen to your instincts and follow through what they are telling you – they're often right.

---

**DEAR JOHN ...**

Dear John,

I'm writing this letter more in sorrow than anger and also to put down some of the things that I may not have clearly said when we talked last night. As I said to you then it seems to me that our relationship has reached a point at which it should — or shouldn't — move on to a greater level of commitment from both of us. We've been going out together now for some two years — two good years in which I've enjoyed almost everything that we've done together. I say 'almost everything' because I didn't enjoy the rows we had — they seemed to me to be destructive and painful. But I did enjoy the many, many good times that we spent in each other's company. These left me feeling that our relationship was capable of handling the stresses and strains of moving up to a greater level of commitment — one that would be bigger and better for both of us. However, from all that you've said, this increased commitment is not one that you're ready to make — at this time. But I need this commitment if I am to have a future with you as a couple. I do acknowledge that this change is not an easy one for you and that you've struggled with it. But, because you can't make it, I must, as I said to you last night, ask you not to get in touch with me again.

I hope that you find what you're looking for.

Alice

---

If you delayed or stalled the other side's walkout then it's time to quickly move on to the other side of your choice – that of trying to recover the situation.

# Recovery

Deadlock and its near cousin, breakdown, are uncomfortable. Nobody enjoys them. They erode or undermine the trust that has painstakingly been built up during the early stages of your negotiation; they bring you face to face with the risk of losing your hoped for outcomes. But, like most things in life, they have, hidden within them, an opportunity. For the way that you handle them will make a significant difference to both the outcome of your negotiation and the way that people see you as a negotiator. Handle them well and it'll be a turning point – for both the negotiation and your career as a negotiator. Handle them badly and both will suffer.

The gateway to success in handling deadlock and breakdown lies in your recovery programme which, like all the other recovery programmes, follows a sequence of steps or stages. The simplest sequence for these is:

**Stage one:** Keep your communications open
**Stage two:** Heal the rift
**Stage three:** Find a way to move forward together.

Let's look at each of these in turn.

## Stage one: keeping your communications open

This, the first stage in your recovery programme, is not just important – it's essential. Without it you've little hope of finding a way back, your negotiation's adrift with no one to throw you a rope. With it, you've the beginnings of something that may lead to a successful outcome. Keeping a communication window open is a must whatever happens – even when the other side stages a walkout. Doing it isn't the easiest of tasks – you may have to swallow your pride, stand back from your feelings – and you'll need to draw on all of the communication skills that you've used during the earlier stages of the negotiation and that you read about in Chapter 7. You might find all this a little easier to understand, and do, if you look at the alternatives: that is, what might happen if you *don't* communicate.

For when you don't keep your communications with the other side open, you'll lose the deal that's on the table, a deal which, while it isn't perfect, is better than what you've got now. You could also find that failure to communicate leads to the other side taking action against you – by going on strike or withdrawing services.

You might find that the other side will make a deal with someone else. If you can live with any or all of these then there seems, on the face of it, little or no reason for you to communicate with them. But there is – first, because you'll need to tell them that conclusion, politely and clearly, and second, because you never know when you'll next be sitting across the negotiating table from them again.

If, however, you're setting out down the road to recovery, the communications with the other side should be aimed at getting them back into talking mode. A letter, an e-mail, a telephone call or an informal lunch – these are all perfectly good ways of effecting a reconciliation. The one that you choose will reflect your relationship with the other side. But, however or wherever it's done, this overture must be:

■ blame-free, and

■ aimed at getting the talking going again.

Once this happens, you're ready to move on to the next stage.

---

**DEAR ALICE ...**

*Dear Alice,*

*It's been a couple of months since you asked me to respect your wish to break off contact between us. In that time I've been doing some thinking – thinking about what I want from my life and, most importantly, about you and I. One of the things that I've realized is how important you are to me.*

*I'd like to be able to talk with you about this and, hopefully, how it might help us to find a way of being together again.*

*Perhaps we could have some lunch together?*

*John*

---

# Stage two: healing the break

It isn't easy to come back into a negotiation, particularly after the disappointment and difficulties of an earlier breakdown in discussions. So, if the other side does agree to restart, first words are important. It is obvious, but nevertheless well worth stating, that these first words should be welcoming, constructive and helpful. Allocating blame or suggesting, however indirectly, that you were right and they were wrong are prime examples of how *not* to do it. What you want to achieve is finding a position or situation in which you can work together to solve a mutual problem. This problem is the obvious one of deciding how you'll move forward. 'One step at a time' is not only a good motto here – it is also a good action plan. Examples of the sorts of questions that you and the other side need to answer and that typically mark the steps you'll take are:

■ Do we want to continue to negotiate together or was the breakdown irretrievable?

■ Can we resolve our difficulties ourselves?

■ Do we need outside help to move forward?

The answers to these and other questions take us into the third and final stage.

# Stage three: finding the way forward

The questions that you've asked and answered in the previous stage will get you off to a flying start here. If you've jointly decided that you can move forward together, then the process is a familiar one. But the offers and counter-offers can only start when you've both been up-front and honest about the issues that pulled you up short before.

Once you've done this, then the sort of tactics that we saw in Chapters 9 and 11 – such as fragmenting, trading concessions, 'splitting the difference' etc. – can get you up and moving. Take care though, for trust is often an early casualty when breakdowns occur and that trust will need to be carefully rebuilt.

If you've jointly decided that you need outside help, the three options available to you are:

■ Conciliation

■ Mediation

■ Arbitration.

We'll look at each of these in turn.

## Conciliation

Conciliation is a voluntary and informal process. The conciliator is an unbiased yet competent person who is accepted by both you and the other side. His or her role will be to focus on making sure that you and the other side really understand each other. The conciliator doesn't make suggestions or propose alternative solutions – he or she merely works towards helping you and the other side to generate your own solutions.

---

**RED OR BLUE?**

Tracey and Steve had been arguing for some time when Craig arrived at their flat. They were decorating the lounge. Tracey wanted the walls to be painted red – ochre red to be exact. Steve wanted to use a blue – duck shell blue to be just as exact. 'What do you think?' they asked him. Craig sighed – this was not a situation he relished. He took a breath. 'What I think doesn't matter,' he said, 'it's what you two think that counts. After all, it's your lounge.' They both looked at him, suspiciously, he thought. 'But I'll try to help you decide together' he said '– after we've had a cup of coffee.'

---

## Mediation

When you choose to go the mediation route you're choosing a process that's more proactive than conciliation. But there are similarities. For example, the process of mediation is also one that's voluntary and informal and uses a third party – a mediator – who is unbiased. But he or she must have the required skills and be acceptable to both you and the other side. What's different is that the mediator will work with you both, not only to make sure that you understand each other, but also, and more importantly, to suggest and develop potential solutions to your deadlock. But, as was so with the process of conciliation, you and the other side aren't bound or obliged by the process to accept these solutions.

---

**RED OR BLUE?**

'How about a nice light purple?' Craig asked – more in desperation than hope.

They both looked at him. 'That's amazing', said Tracey, 'why didn't we think of that!' 'Yeah, far out', muttered Steve, 'that's a real cool colour!' Craig winced – 'Still', he thought, 'it was the first time they'd agreed about any colour in the last hour.'

---

## Arbitration

Conciliation and mediation are, as you've seen above, both informal and free from any obligation to accept the potential solutions developed. But this situation changes when you move into arbitration. For arbitration is a formal process – involving an independent professional body, expert, tribunal or court – and both you and the other side are bound to accept its findings. The arbitrator is, of course, independent, competent and informed and she, he or they will hear both sides of the story independently and in confidence. The verdict reached is handed down to only you and the other side. All this formality brings with it the security of knowing that your case – which might contain confidential information – will not be exposed to the public gaze. But the downside of arbitration is that it is a slow and expensive process. For that reason, it is generally only used in complex negotiations with high consequential costs.

## What next?

Reaching and recovering an agreement is not enough – you have to be able to implement that agreement. The next chapter looks at the ways and means of doing just that.

## Checklist ✔

In this chapter you have seen that:

- ■ negotiations can become deadlocked or fail for a number of reasons.                                                    ☐

■ walking out of a negotiation is sometimes necessary. ☐

■ when you walk, do it:
   – after you've recovered your cool and prepared both yourself and your exit statement ☐
   – after you've told the other side:
      • where you are ☐
      • where you see that they are ☐
      • why it won't work ☐
   – quietly and calmly. ☐

■ when somebody walks out on you, use your instinct to tell you whether to try to stop them or to let them go. ☐

■ the three-stage programme for recovery from a deadlock is:
   **Stage one:** keep your communications open ☐
   **Stage two:** heal the rift ☐
   **Stage three:** find a way to move forward together. ☐

■ if you need outside help you can use:
   – conciliation ☐
   – mediation ☐
   or
   – arbitration. ☐

# 13 | IMPLEMENTATION

*The thrill ain't in the winning, it's in the doing.*

**Chuck Noll**

So, here you are. One way or another, you've got to your agreement. To do that you've used conflict constructively and, as a result, you've reached – with the other side – an outcome that you're both happy about. But that agreement – vital as it is – isn't enough. For if your negotiation is going to reach an outcome that's a lasting and stable success, you have to be able to implement what you've agreed. That is, you have to convert the words of your agreement into deeds, you have to be able to fulfil its promise, perform its actions, carry out its details. The gap between where you are now and that, between the words and the deeds, is, not surprisingly, called the 'implementation gap'. For some of your negotiations this gap will be both brief and small. In the market place, for example, you'll agree a price and then – almost straight away – you and the other side will exchange money and goods. But in other of your negotiations this gap will be wide and full of obstacles and delays. Questions such as 'who does what?', 'when or where will it be done?' and 'how will it be done?' will need to be answered before you can attempt to bridge this implementation gap and reach the goal of fulfilment. Finding the answers to these questions and then using them to bridge this gap is not an optional, take-it-or-leave it extra in the ways and means of your negotiations. For if you fail to convert the brave words of your agreement into concrete and realistic actions, then failure will loom. One of the most effective ways of avoiding this is to treat the implementation of your agreement as a project.

# Projects, projects and projects

The word 'project' has become a commonplace part of all our vocabularies. Our children do projects as part of their schoolwork. You and I create, plan and implement our own individual projects – such as moving house, having an extension or a deck built, organizing a holiday, losing weight or even choosing and buying a new car. Our communities have projects such as raising funds for church repairs, famine relief for Africa or new computers for the village school. But most of the projects that we meet in our lives occur in our workplaces. These, like the projects of our homes, schools and communities, show considerable diversity. They can be about almost anything – a new office block or factory, changing the way things are done, the introduction of a quality manual, creating a new product, changing people's behaviour or influencing their views about one issue or another. They can vary considerably in the number of people involved, the activities they need, their implementation cost and the time required to achieve completion. Yet, despite all this variety, all of these projects do have characteristics in common.

# What is a project?

Your experience and what you've seen above will have told you that a project can:

> be large or small
> ■ involve any number of people
> last for years or days
> have almost anything as an outcome.

But these aren't the only characteristics that a project has. For projects also have:

> outcomes that are unique and defined
> time-spans or durations that are limited
> endpoints or completion dates that are defined
> activities that create change and use a variety of resources.

This tells you that projects are about creating one-offs – rather than copies or duplicates – and that they aim to do that by a particular point in time and by consuming or using a variety of transient resources. It also tells you that once the project's outcome is created then the project ceases to exist, the people involved in its creation will move on to other jobs or projects and the outcome itself will become part of another day-to-day operation. As you can see, these characteristics make the project a very different animal to the sorts of things that you usually meet in your routine day-to-day activities. So how does a project help you to bridge the implementation gap of your negotiated agreement?

# Bridging the gap

If you're going to build that bridge to take your negotiated agreement from the safety of the negotiating room into the realities of the outside world, then there are three things that you must have. These – the keys to all successful projects – are:

- a programme or plan
- a team
- a monitoring, control and information system.

Without these, you'll fail and your bridge – reaching out from agreement to fulfilment – will never reach the other side. With them, you'll be able to plan, implement, monitor and control all of the actions that will take you to success. For these three – programme, team and system – lie at the heart of all projects. As such they are key to the project that has as its outcome the successful implementation of your negotiated agreement.

# Programmes and plans

A project programme or plan is quite a sophisticated tool. It converts the words of your agreement into a detailed sequence of interdependent actions and activities. That plan, however, is far more than just a list of those activities. For, during its creation and use, it will also provide:

a common understanding, for all involved, of what actions and resources are required

a basis for co-operative effort between you and the other side

a base-line for the monitoring of the implementation project

an overarching view of that project.

In order to provide these the plan must be:

clear and specific in its content

easily understood by all who use or see it

agreed by you and the other side

capable of accepting changes at both a detailed and broad level, and

capable of being used to monitor what's actually happening.

Your journey towards the creation of this plan starts with the steps of identifying:

what activities are to be undertaken

when those activities are to be started and finished, and

what people, equipment, tools or other resources are needed.

For example, if your negotiation has generated an agreement about a raise in rates of pay for some of the people who work in your organization, then its implementation will involve the activities of:

identifying all of the individuals who are to be paid more

changing the base-rate data used to calculate their wages

trial running and checking calculations

calculating any back-pay

generating realistic target dates for start and completion of these activities.

Similarly, when you've agreed the price that you'll pay for your new house, the plan for implementing that agreement will contain such actions as:

- identifying fixtures and fittings to be included in the sale
- finding out about legal constraints on the use of the property
- checking to see if there are any developments planned – such as a new by-pass or a high-rise block of flats – in the area adjacent to the property
- generating any finance needed
- generating draft and agreeing contracts
- exchanging and completing contracts
- generating target dates for the start and finish of these and other activities.

These activities will be undertaken by yourself or people that you employ who have the required skills and knowledge. They will involve the use of resources such as computers, software, pro-forma contracts etc.

The act of listing these activities and their people and resource demands will begin to give you a sense of how your implementation project might be planned and controlled. It is worth, for example, asking yourself whether the activities listed are in the right order or whether you could save time or money by doing them in a different order or by using different resources. The next step in the planning process is to:

- estimate the time taken for these activities
- identify their dependency patterns.

At this, the initial stage of your planning, your estimates of the time taken for the activities involved need only be concerned with the relative duration of the activities. Experience, or the advice of other people who've done it before, will tell you which are the activities with the longest durations and which activities are linked together in dependency patterns. A simple example of these dependency patterns can be found when you look at the activities that must be completed before you can boil water in an electric kettle. The water cannot boil until the kettle has been:

- filled with water
- plugged in, and

the electric power has been switched on.

That is, the activity of 'boiling the water' is dependant upon the completion of the activities of 'filling the kettle', 'plugging in the kettle', and 'switching on the electric power' – all of these have to be completed before it can take place. Once you've worked out these dependency patterns and made an initial estimate of the durations of the activities, you can generate the first draft of your plan – a draft that you'll revise and update as more and better information becomes available. What you have to decide next is what sort of plan you are going to use.

# Networks and bar charts

Earlier in this chapter you saw that the plan that you use must be:

    clear and specific in its content

    easily understood by all who use or see it

    capable of accepting changes at both a detailed and broad level, and

    capable of being used to monitor what's actually happening.

The simplest forms of the project plan that will do this for you are:

    the Gantt chart, and

    The Critical Path network.

However, a detailed study of these and other more sophisticated planning tools is beyond the scope of this book. To do that you'll need to branch out into more specialized texts – some of which are mentioned in the Further Reading section on page 174. But we can take a look, albeit briefly, at their pros and cons.

## Gantt charts

The Gantt chart was developed in 1917 by an American engineer called Henry Gantt. It is based on the use of a horizontal line for each activity on a time-based chart with the length of the line representing the time taken to complete that activity. All of the lines are displayed on a single chart whose horizontal axis is divided into units of time as in Figure 13.1.

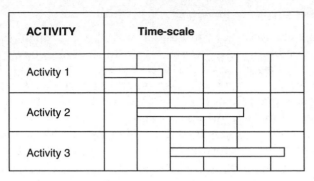

**Figure 13.1   Gantt chart**

The Gantt chart can use a time-scale based on minutes, hours, days or even weeks, depending upon the time-scale of your project, and provides you with a picture of your project. It is a picture that can be easily understood, that shows the relationships of the various activities, and can be used to monitor progress by the filling in of activity lines:

It can also be used to indicate key project points or milestones by the use of symbols such as ◆ in the chart. The Gantt chart is probably the most popular of the project planning methods. It is easily understood and can be presented in a variety of physical forms ranging from a proprietary wall chart using adhesive strips, through the hard copy output of modern computer software, to a hand-drawn chart. The ease and speed with which it can be updated is high, particularly with the wall chart or computer-produced charts. Another of its major advantages lies in the ease with which it can be generated – often needing very limited prior training. However, Gantt charts cannot deal easily with complex projects or with projects which contain high levels of uncertainty about durations or completion times. These, as you'll now see, are best dealt with by the other major type of project planning tool.

## Critical Path networks

There are various types of Critical Path network, the best known using acronyms such as PERT (Programme Evaluation and Review Technique), CPM (Critical Path Method), CPS (Critical Path Scheduling) and CPA (Critical Path Analysis). All of these use networks to display both the order of and connections between the activities of the project. The most easily understood of these is the Activity on Arrow network – a network in which an activity is represented by an arrow. This arrow begins at the start of the activity and ends when it's complete and the network looks like Figure 13.2.

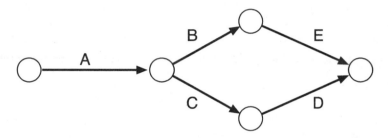

**Figure 13.2    Activity on Arrow network**

The nodes or circles at the start and finish of each activity are, in a completed network, used to record further information and the arrows can also be used to indicate whether the activities are interdependent or whether they are part of the sequence of activities that defines the overall project duration – called the project 'critical path'.

While network-based planning tools are more complex in both their construction and operation than the Gantt chart, they do enable you to quickly examine the implications of changes that occur. This means that you can make decisions about changes based on a good understanding of their implications and examine the trade-offs between cost, time and money. However, the network plan has less visual impact than the Gantt chart and requires considerable training and experience for it to be used efficiently. For these reasons it is used, often in its computer-driven form, on large and complex projects. But, whether you choose a Critical Path network or Gantt chart, the plan you create is really just the beginning of the implementation project. To implement that plan what you need is a team.

# Teams

The word 'team' is a very common one. We have teams on our sports fields – as in football, soccer, rugby, baseball and basketball teams – and teams in our workplaces – as in 'Finishing shop team' or 'Telephone sales team'. When we look it up in the dictionary, we find the word 'team' is defined by phrases like 'a number of people' and verbs such as 'collaborating' and 'working together'. Teams generally have members with defined functional roles, such as 'goalkeeper', 'pitcher' or 'team leader', and what goes on inside them is often seen to be co-operative and constructive – as in 'team spirit' or 'team work'. In all sorts of situations – at work, at play, and in the home – the team has a proven track-record of creativity and achievement. Most of us have experienced, at some point in our lives, that extra 'something' that a good team can create. A team that works well can, sometimes literally, 'move mountains'.

The team that you use to implement your negotiated agreement should be no less an animal and in order to reach this peak of performance it should be made up of people:

■ from both sides of the negotiation
■ who have:
　　– higher than average functional skills
　　– sensitivity to the 'politics' of the project
　　– strong problem-solving skills.

The team leader or project manager is an important role in this team – often making the difference between success and failure – and 'partnership' is a key word in the way the team operates. The conflict of the negotiation is over; now it is time to make sure that the agreement is implemented – successfully. Teams that do this well have members who act together in ways that are co-operative and aimed at generating outcomes that are desired by the whole team, rather than any one individual. These teams are task focused. Their leadership is less formal, even to the point of being shared, with the leader role moving around the team as the availability of individuals or the phase of task in hand changes. Their meetings are usually open-ended, untidy debates aimed at solving problems. All of this provides you – and the other side – with a way to tap into and harness the efforts, skills, abilities and creativity of all who are involved. The team has a considerable potential to contribute to the success of your implementation project. But even the best of teams needs a framework on which to focus its efforts and this is where we find your project's monitoring, control and information system.

## Monitoring, control and information systems

The activities of your implementation project won't always happen in the way or at the time that you plan them to. The way to counteract the difficulties that arise from these diversions from your plan lies in the way that you create and use your implementation project monitoring and control system. When created and used with care, this system will identify the project's drifts and divergences and provide you with what you need to put your project back 'on-line'.

When you monitor your project you'll measure, record, collate and analyse data about its activities. This data will tell you things like whether a particular activity is on schedule or whether it is delayed. In more sophisticated monitoring systems, it will also tell you about the cost and resource usage of activities and whether – or not – these are in line with your budgeted usage. It is important that this data is both relevant and credible as well as being timely and understandable. To be effective, your project monitoring must provide you with active information. Not only must it give you the answers to questions such as 'Is this activity on schedule?', 'Have we overspent the project budget?' or 'What is the project's probable finish date?' – it must also tell you about the where and when of your project's drifts and deviations. For, when you have this information, then you can move on to another vital element in the management of your implementation project – that of controlling it.

Project control is aimed at reducing the gap between what is actually happening and what you planned should happen. As such, it is rooted in the data generated by your project monitoring. To be effective, its actions should be appropriate, quick and cost-effective. Getting these actions right can take real skill and judgement – because there's often never enough data or time. But whatever you do, it must be based on what facts you have – rather than on your opinions – and be targeted solely towards keeping the project in line with your plan.

Once your implementation project is underway, once its monitoring and controlling systems are active, you'll soon come across another of the factors that is crucial to its success – that of effective communication.

Most of this communication is about the what, how and why of the project's progress, and most of it involves passing information to people who aren't actively involved in the implementation project. One of the ways that you can do this is by progress reports. These need to be issued regularly, though they can also be issued when a special event or problem warrants it. Their primary purpose is to report the general progress of the project and so they should be understandable, concise and based on facts. They are generally read by busy people, so brevity is also desirable. Supporting data, where required, should be nested in appendices. Routine progress reports – in the form of tables of figures, Gantt charts or Activity on Arrow networks – should be presented with limited comment. These reports are often complementary to another method of reporting project progress – that of the project meeting.

Project meetings are important. They are the arena within which the people with a direct interest in the project's progress exert their influence. As such they, like the negotiations that preceded them, possess a considerable potential for conflict and disagreement. Because of this, your project meetings must be conducted in ways that are clearly and effectively focused on the achievement of results and targets. Managing a project meeting that achieves these objectives represents a real skill on the part of the project manager, and agendas – that state the business to be discussed, minutes – that briefly record what was decided and who is to do what, and briefing papers, such as project progress reports – all play their part in this. The best project meetings are brief – no longer than $1^1/_2$ hours – and events from which you and the other side emerge better informed about the project, having been involved in decisions on key project issues and with a better understanding of your and their role in the implementation project. These meetings should involve no more than ten people and should be chaired with skill and sensitivity. In the end, a project meeting is only as good as the people who attend. If the meeting is to be valuable and effective, then these people must be willing to engage in a constructive dialogue with each other. Given that, and an experienced and capable chairperson, the meetings of your project will help your monitoring and your controlling.

## What next?

Now you will move on to the final part of this book – Part Four. In this you will review all the key issues identified in the previous chapters and take the opportunity to assess your own performance as a negotiator.

## Checklist ☑

In this chapter you have seen that:

■ some of the agreements you make in your negotiations are implemented with little or no indecision or delay. ☐

■ in other negotiations the gap between agreement and implementation is wide and full of obstacles and delays. ☐

■ one of the most effective ways of bridging this gap is to treat this implementation as a project. ☐

■ projects can:
 – be large or small ☐
 – involve any number of people ☐

      – last for years or days                                                    ☐

      – have almost anything as an outcome.                         ☐

■ all projects have:

      – outcomes that are unique and defined                         ☐

      – time-spans or durations that are limited                     ☐

      – endpoints or completion dates that are defined     ☐

      – activities that create change and use a variety of
        resources.                                                                        ☐

■ to be effective your implementation project will need:

      – a programme or plan                                                    ☐

      – a team                                                                            ☐

      – a monitoring, control and information system.           ☐

■ project plans need to be:

      – clear and specific in their content                               ☐

      – easily understood by all who use or see them         ☐

      – agreed by you and the other side                              ☐

      – capable of accepting changes at both a detailed
        and broad level                                                                ☐

      – capable of being used to monitor what's actually
        happening.                                                                       ☐

■ creating your implementation plan starts with you
identifying:

      – what activities are to be undertaken                         ☐

      – when those activities are to be started and
        finished                                                                             ☐

      – what people and what equipment, tools or other
        resources are needed                                                      ☐

      – which activities are interdependent.                         ☐

■ the simplest forms of project plan are:

      – Gantt chart                                                                    ☐

      – Critical Path network.                                                   ☐

■ your implementation team should be made up of
people:
- from both sides of the negotiation ☐
- who have:
- higher than average functional skills ☐
- sensitivity to the 'politics' of the project ☐
- strong problem-solving skills. ☐
■ your monitoring, control and information system
should enable you to:
- find out what's happening in your implementation
project ☐
- reduce the gap between that and what you planned
should happen ☐
- keep all the people informed who need to know
about the progress of this project by using project
meetings and progress reports. ☐

## Part Four
# REFLECTIONS

*It is good to have an end to journey toward; but it is the journey that matters, in the end.*

Ursula K. Le Guin

*Somebody showed it to me and I found it by myself.*

Lew Welch

# 14 | KEY POINTS

*Life is rather like a tin of sardines, we're all of us looking for the key.*

**Alan Bennett**

Whatever our jobs and whatever the detail of our days, we are all users when it comes to the process of negotiating. The aim of this book has been to provide you, its reader, with a basic, yet comprehensive, introduction to the ways and means of that process. The chapters that you've read to get to this point were divided up in three parts; parts aimed respectively at helping you to prepare, carry out and complete your negotiations. The objective of this, the final part of the book, is to:

■ summarize, in this chapter, the key issues of negotiating, and

■ give you, in the final chapter, an opportunity to check out where you've got to in your learning process.

## Key issues

### Negotiating

■ negotiating is something that we all do, all of the time

■ negotiations take place about almost everything in our lives

■ negotiation is the most effective way of resolving conflict

■ all negotiations have six core characteristics:
  - they involve people who act either as individuals, representatives, singly or in groups
  - they have the thread of conflict running through them
  - they use bargaining or bartering so you can exchange things
  - they almost always involve face-to-face contact
  - they are about the future
  - they arrive, if successful, at a jointly-taken decision
■ negotiation can be defined as the way that people identify mutually acceptable decisions and agree the what and how of future actions.

## Objectives

■ preparation is key to the success of your negotiations
■ the first step that you take in your preparation is to decide what it is that you *need* rather than want
■ the second is to identify and prioritize the key features of what you need
■ the third step is to research, research and research
■ the final step of this stage of your preparation is to decide what are your ideal, minimum and realistic values.

## The Other Side

■ people are key to your negotiations
■ you need to get to know as much as you can about the people on the other side of your negotiations
■ the other side also has needs
■ the ways that they behave can be partially described by degrees of introversion or extroversion
■ another framework for describing the way people behave uses the way that they use their senses, intuition, thinking and feelings

you need to find out as much as you can about:
- how the other side did it before – their negotiating history
- how they might do it in your future negotiations
- their motives and hidden agendas.

## Strategies and tactics

the strategy you adopt for your negotiations should be designed to link together or unify all that you do in that negotiation

the tactics that you use will be concerned with things like the detail of your actions and responses to the other side's ploys

negotiating is something that you do *with* someone – not *to* them

you'll need to decide:
- whether you go it alone or as part of a team of negotiators
- the order and content of your 'things to do' list for your negotiations
- what tactics you will use

negotiating teams need to be carefully chosen and well prepared

different negotiations need different tactics

an aggressive negotiator will only gain the upper hand if you allow him or her to.

## Where, when and how

negotiations can take place in:
- your space, or
- the other side's space, or
- a neutral space

each of these has its advantages and disadvantages

the ways you use and arrange those spaces are important

- the timing, pace and style of your negotiation can make major contributions to its outcome
- the style that works best is one that's close to your natural one
- that style uses the Three Cs:
  - Considered
  - Careful
  - Calm
- all of these have their roots in your preparation, but being Calm also means being:
  - alert
  - relaxed
  - comfortable.

## Communicating

- most of us could communicate better
- effective, focused communication:
  - can be learnt
  - is a two-way dynamic process
  - requires thought and planning
  - involves the choice of the 'right' medium and channel
- effective communication will only happen if you've thought through and done something about:
  - the needs of the people you're communicating with
  - what might cause it to fail
- most negotiations use the spoken word
- the words that you speak are a direct and flexible way of communicating
- the words you speak are complimented and supported by your 'body language'
- your gestures, facial expressions, movements, postures, gaze and appearance are all part of your body language

■ good negotiating needs good communication.

## Assertion

■ conflict is core to your negotiations
■ most of us find conflict very uncomfortable – it makes us anxious, stressed, uneasy
■ you can choose the way that you respond to this stress
■ you can be:
  – aggressive, or
  – submissive, or
  – assertive
■ effective balanced assertion involves 'standing up' for one's own rights without 'violating' another's rights
■ achieving this sort of assertion involves you in:
  – learning its skilful use
  – being effective in your communications
  – taking the risk that it may not produce the result you want
  – exercising your judgement about when and where you use it
■ Cool negotiating involves you in using the three S's:
  – Spotting what's happening
  – Stepping away from the anger
  – Speaking assertively.

## Opening, talking, listening and proposing

■ open your negotiation by being:
  – pleasant
  – firm
  – assertive
■ you and the other side will, at least, share:
  – a desire to reach an agreement
  – a wish to do that as pleasantly as possible
■ your opening proposal can be suggestions about the agenda of your negotiation

■ this agenda will give you the bridge you need to move to your first agreement

■ when you make your opening proposal make sure that you:
- leave room for manoeuvre
- indicate any conditions attached to it
- seek their reactions to it
- don't make any:
  - concessions
  - exclusions
  - unrealistic or extreme offers

■ it is important to respond to the other side's proposal carefully, asking for further information or more time if you need them

■ it is vital to listen effectively

■ when you ask questions make sure that they're:
- open, or
- probing

■ make sure you discuss proposals in ways that are:
- cool
- calm
- constructive
- effective.

## The Bargaining Zone

■ bargaining is something we all do

■ the act of bargaining lies at the heart of your negotiation

■ you cross the boundaries of the Bargaining Zone when:
- you make your first proposal, or
- respond – with a counter-proposal – to the other side's first proposal.

■ the Bargaining Zone contains:
- the Buyer's:

- Ideal Offer
- Realistic Offer
- Highest Offer
- and the Seller's
  - Ideal Price
  - Realistic Price
  - Lowest Price

in the Bargaining Zone:
- the Seller's Opening Price is considerably more than the Buyer's Opening Offer
- the Seller's Ideal Price is quite a lot more than the Buyer's Ideal Offer
- the Seller's Realistic Price is more than the Buyer's Realistic Offer

in order to reach an agreement there must be an overlap between the other side's and your value range so that the Buyer's Highest Offer is greater than the Seller's Lowest Price

moving your negotiation forward – from general to the specific, or from the explored to the proposed – requires you to choose and use the right tactic.

this tactic should move you and the other side closer together, to find ways of increasing the opportunities for agreement

tactics you can use include:
- fragmenting
- what if?
- concession and trade
- hard work and commitment
- variables and options
- by-passing
- periodic summaries
- saving face

the tactic you use must be a matter for your own judgement.

## Negotiating skills

most of us draw on our experience to tell us what to do in a negotiation

■ good negotiators:
- get results
- gets results where and when they are needed
- do so by being, amongst other things, adaptable
■ effective negotiators behave in ways that:
- use words carefully
- give notice of what they're about to do
- give reasons first, then conclusions
- use summaries and testing a lot
- use open-ended and probing questions
- express their feelings, but do so coolly
■ effective negotiators don't:
- use words carelessly or to irritate
- use 'knee-jerk' responses
- get drawn into attacks and counter-attacks
- dilute arguments
- give conclusions first, then reasons.

## Agreeing and closing

■ the jump from offer to decision to agreement takes place in the Final Offer Zone
■ the boundaries of that zone lie at your and the other side's realistic offer and price values
■ moving from your realistic price into the Final Offer Zone follows your review of your negotiation
■ getting to an agreement takes:
- patience, skill and ability
- the skilful use of actions such as summarizing, revisiting earlier issues, making concessions, offering to 'split the difference', presenting alternatives or sewing everything together
- good timing
■ to close effectively you need to:
- be open to closure from the very beginning of your negotiation

- make it clear that this *is* your final offer
- present your offer in an upbeat and confident manner
- leave the other side some space to review your final offer

if they say 'No' or haggle – move out

■ if they say 'Yes' – put it in a written form that's:

| | |
|---|---|
| – brief | – concise |
| – factual | – accurate. |

## Breakdown and deadlock

negotiations can become deadlocked or fail for a number of reasons

walking out of a negotiation is sometimes necessary

when you walk, do it:

- after you've recovered your cool and prepared both yourself and your exit statement
- after you've told the other side:
  - where you are
  - where you see that they are
  - why it won't work
- quietly and calmly

when somebody walks on you, use your instinct to tell you whether to try to stop them or to let them go

the three-stage programme for recovery from a deadlock is:

**Stage one:** keep your communications open

**Stage two:** heal the rift

**Stage three:** find a way to move forward together

if you need outside help you can use:

- conciliation
- mediation, or
- arbitration.

# Implementation

■ some of the agreements you make in your negotiations are implemented with little or no indecision or delay

■ in other negotiations the gap between agreement and implementation is wide and full of obstacles and delays

■ one of the most effective ways of bridging this gap is to treat this implementation as a project

■ projects can:
  – be large or small
  – involve any number of people
  – last for years or days
  – have almost anything as an outcome

■ all projects have:
  – outcomes that are unique and defined
  – time-spans or durations that are limited
  – endpoints or completion dates that are defined
  – activities that create change and use a variety of resources

■ to be effective your implementation project will need:
  – a programme or plan
  – a team
  – a monitoring, control and information system

■ project plans need to be:
  – clear and specific in their content
  – easily understood by all who use or see them
  – agreed by you and the other side
  – capable of accepting changes at both a detailed and broad level
  – capable of being used to monitor what's actually happening

■ creating your implementation plan starts with you identifying:
  – what activities are to be undertaken
  – when those activities are to be started and finished

  – what people and what equipment, tools or other
    resources are needed
  – which activities are interdependent
■ the simplest forms of project plan are:
  – Gantt chart
  – Critical Path network
■ your implementation team should be made up of
  people:
  – from both sides of the negotiation
  – who have:
    • higher than average functional skills
    • sensitivity to the 'politics' of the project
    • strong problem-solving skills
■ your monitoring, control and information system
  should enable you to:
  – find out what's happening in your implementation
    project
  – reduce the gap between that and what you planned
    should happen
  – keep all the people informed who need to know
    about the  progress of this project by using project
    meetings and progress reports.

# What next ?

Next, we come to the final chapter of this book – one in which you
will have the opportunity to check out where you've got to in your
journey to becoming an effective negotiator.

# 15 ASSESSING WHERE YOU ARE

*This is not the end. It is not even the beginning of the end.*

*But it is, perhaps, the end of the beginning.*

**Winston Churchill**

As you approach the end of this book, it is worth reminding yourself about the aim or objective of your journey through its pages. That aim has been, quite simply, to gain access to the tools and skills that will enable you to negotiate well. The detail of this journey has been mapped out in the fourteen chapters that preceded this one. It has all been there for you – the preparation, the research, the strategy and tactics, the opening, the doing, the closing and the implementing. It has been, as they say, the journey of a lifetime. For being an effective negotiator isn't just a workplace skill, it is a skill that colours, flavours, influences the way we live all of our lives. It is, to use the jargon of the social psychologists, the ultimate 'transferable' skill. But making the shift up to being an effective negotiator isn't one of those overnight tasks; it takes perseverance, patience, time and effort to move on up. But what can help you on that journey – from where you are to where you want to be – are targets. The Negotiation Check Out Questionnaire given in this chapter is designed to help you to set those targets for yourself. You should use it to identify your strengths and find your weaknesses. Use it to generate change, to set targets and measure your movement towards achieving them. Use it to support and focus your progress towards becoming an effective negotiator.

# The Negotiation Check Out questionnaire

For each of the statements made below, ring the answer that is closest to the way you feel about what's said. Don't think about what the 'right' answer might be – ring the one that feels right for you. When you've finished each page, add up your score and put it in the box at the bottom of the page. When you've answered them all, transfer your scores to the boxes on page 173. Then take a look at the Analysis on that page to see how well – or badly – you're doing.

| | EVERY TIME | MOST OF THE TIME | SOMETIMES | NOT OFTEN | NEVER |
|---|---|---|---|---|---|
| **1** I recognize and use the opportunities that I have to negotiate | 1 | 2 | 3 | 4 | 5 |
| **2** I try to use negotiation to resolve conflict situations | 1 | 2 | 3 | 4 | 5 |
| **3** I want my negotiations to create an agreement that we all accept | 1 | 2 | 3 | 4 | 5 |
| **4** I prepare for my negotiations | 1 | 2 | 3 | 4 | 5 |
| **5** I start that preparation by: | | | | | |
| ■ deciding what I really need as an outcome | 1 | 2 | 3 | 4 | 5 |
| ■ working out what are, for me, the key features of that outcome | 1 | 2 | 3 | 4 | 5 |
| ■ prioritizing those features | 1 | 2 | 3 | 4 | 5 |
| **6** I find out everything I can about that outcome | 1 | 2 | 3 | 4 | 5 |
| **7** I decide what are the ideal, minimum and realistic values that I place upon that outcome | 1 | 2 | 3 | 4 | 5 |

Page Total

| | EVERY TIME | MOST OF THE TIME | SOMETIMES | NOT OFTEN | NEVER |
|---|---|---|---|---|---|
| **8** I find out all I can about the other side's: | | | | | |
| ■ needs | 1 | 2 | 3 | 4 | 5 |
| ■ ways of negotiating | 1 | 2 | 3 | 4 | 5 |
| ■ history of negotiating | 1 | 2 | 3 | 4 | 5 |
| ■ likely approach in this negotiation | 1 | 2 | 3 | 4 | 5 |
| ■ motives and hidden agendas | 1 | 2 | 3 | 4 | 5 |
| **9** I work out what the right strategy is for each negotiation | 1 | 2 | 3 | 4 | 5 |
| **10** I think carefully about whether I'll negotiate on my own or as part of a team | 1 | 2 | 3 | 4 | 5 |
| **11** I review and rehearse the tactics that I'll use | 1 | 2 | 3 | 4 | 5 |
| **12** I make sure that these tactics are right for this negotiation | 1 | 2 | 3 | 4 | 5 |
| **13** I make sure that I'm ready to handle an aggressive negotiator | 1 | 2 | 3 | 4 | 5 |
| **14** I choose the location of my negotiation and its layout carefully, and agree it with the other side | 1 | 2 | 3 | 4 | 5 |
| **15** I make sure that the style I adopt when I negotiate is one that I'm comfortable with | 1 | 2 | 3 | 4 | 5 |
| **16** I do all I can to make sure that I'm relaxed | 1 | 2 | 3 | 4 | 5 |
| **17** I take into account what I want to achieve and who I'm talking to when I communicate with the other side | 1 | 2 | 3 | 4 | 5 |
| **18** I try to anticipate and overcome difficulties | 1 | 2 | 3 | 4 | 5 |
| **19** I enjoy talking with – rather than to or at – people | 1 | 2 | 3 | 4 | 5 |

Page Total

|  | EVERY TIME | MOST OF THE TIME | SOMETIMES | NOT OFTEN | NEVER |
|---|---|---|---|---|---|
| **20** I try to listen | 1 | 2 | 3 | 4 | 5 |
| **21** I try to listen without bias or prejudice and to really hear what's being said | 1 | 2 | 3 | 4 | 5 |
| **22** I try to be aware of the impact that my body language has on others | 1 | 2 | 3 | 4 | 5 |
| **23** I keep myself aware of other people's body language | 1 | 2 | 3 | 4 | 5 |
| **24** I try to persuade openly, doing it with somebody rather than to them | 1 | 2 | 3 | 4 | 5 |
| **25** I choose, even in the face of aggression to be assertive, rather than aggressive or passive | 1 | 2 | 3 | 4 | 5 |
| **26** I work hard at using assertiveness skilfully, appropriately and effectively | 1 | 2 | 3 | 4 | 5 |
| **27** I realize that the way I open my negotiation is important and work hard at getting it right | 1 | 2 | 3 | 4 | 5 |
| **28** I try hard to identify or establish the common ground that I share with the other side | 1 | 2 | 3 | 4 | 5 |
| **29** When I make a proposal I make sure that's done: | | | | | |
| ■ at the right time | 1 | 2 | 3 | 4 | 5 |
| ■ in a way that leaves room for manoeuvre, and | 1 | 2 | 3 | 4 | 5 |
| ■ that it doesn't contain concessions or exclusions | 1 | 2 | 3 | 4 | 5 |
| **30** I listen carefully to the Other Side's proposals and chose, with care, the tactic that I use to move us both towards agreement | 1 | 2 | 3 | 4 | 5 |
| **31** I watch out for and respond to decision signals | 1 | 2 | 3 | 4 | 5 |

Page Total

| | EVERY TIME | MOST OF THE TIME | SOMETIMES | NOT OFTEN | NEVER |
|---|---|---|---|---|---|
| **32** I practise and use the Do's of effective negotiating | 1 | 2 | 3 | 4 | 5 |
| **33** I avoid using the Don'ts of effective negotiating | 1 | 2 | 3 | 4 | 5 |
| **34** I look for closure from the beginning of the negotiation | 1 | 2 | 3 | 4 | 5 |
| **35** I make my final offer in a way that confirms that it's final | 1 | 2 | 3 | 4 | 5 |
| **36** If a negotiation becomes deadlocked, I take time out to check out whether it is – or isn't – time to walk | 1 | 2 | 3 | 4 | 5 |
| **37** When I try to recover from a deadlock I: | | | | | |
| ■ keep communications open | 1 | 2 | 3 | 4 | 5 |
| ■ try to find a way to heal the rift | 1 | 2 | 3 | 4 | 5 |
| ■ find a way forward | 1 | 2 | 3 | 4 | 5 |
| **38** I'm willing to use conciliation or mediation or arbitration to find a way forward | 1 | 2 | 3 | 4 | 5 |
| **39** When there's a risk of delay in implementing an agreement I'm willing to treat this task as a project | 1 | 2 | 3 | 4 | 5 |
| **40** My implementation projects have: | | | | | |
| ■ plans | 1 | 2 | 3 | 4 | 5 |
| ■ teams, and | 1 | 2 | 3 | 4 | 5 |
| ■ monitoring, control and information systems | 1 | 2 | 3 | 4 | 5 |

Page Total

My total was: ☐ on page 169

and ☐ on page 170

and ☐ on page 171

and ☐ on page 172

giving a total of ☐

## Analysis

If your score is **52–104**:  You're negotiating very well – keep it up!

**105–156**:  You're negotiating well but with some areas of uncertainty. Identify the areas where you scored 3s and 2s, re-read the relevant chapter and set yourself targets for improvement.

**157–208**:  There seem to be some problems here. Pick out your highest scoring areas and try to identify what's going wrong. Then go back to the relevant chapter and read it again – slowly. Map out a performance improvement programme and keep to it.

**209–260**:  **YOU CAN'T BE SERIOUS!**

You really must get hold of the idea that negotiation is something that you do *with* people – rather than to them. Try to listen to feedback, identify your mistakes one at a time and use them to learn from.

# FURTHER READING

## Books

This list of books is intended to help you extend your knowledge about negotiating. As you will continue to add to and refine this knowledge throughout the rest of your life it can only be a list that 'push starts' your own process. Because the act of negotiation reaches into all the nooks and crannies of our lives, the range – and sometimes the depth – of these books goes beyond those of the usual 'how to' book. Some of the books (marked *) may be out of print but are well worth the search to find a copy on the shelves of your second-hand book shop or local, college or university libraries.

### Arbitration, conciliation and mediation

Fisher, T., *National Family Guide to Separation and Divorce*, 1997, Century Hutchinson
International Labour Organisation, *Conciliation in Labour Disputes*, 1988, ILO
Kennerley, J.A., *Arbitration*, 1994, Pitman
Moore, C.W., *The Mediation Process*, 1996, Prentice Hall
Zeigler Jr, J.W., *The Mediation Kit*, 1997, Wiley

### Assertion

Back, K. and Back, K., *Assertiveness at Work*, 1999, McGraw-Hill,

### Bargaining

Morley, I.E. and Stephenson, G.M., *The Social Psychology of Bargaining*, 1977, Allen and Unwin *

## Consumer information

Consumer Reports, *The Consumer Reports Buying Guide 2000*, Consumer Reports Books (reprinted annually)
Consumer Reports, *The Consumer Reports 2000 Car Buying Guide,* Consumer Reports Books (reprinted annually)
Consumers Association, *Which?* magazine, published monthly.

## Communication

Baguley, P., *Effective Communication for Modern Business,* (1994), McGraw-Hill *
Heller, R., *Communicate Clearly*, 1998, Dorling Kindersley
Thomsett, M.C., *The Little Black Book of Business Meetings,* 1989, McGraw-Hill
Wainwright, G.R., *Teach Yourself Body Language*, 1999, Hodder & Stoughton

## Negotiating across cultures

Fang, A., *Chinese Business Negotiating Style*, 1998, Sage
Foster, D., *Bargaining across Borders*, 1995, McGraw-Hill
Hendon, D.W. and others, *Cross-Cultural Negotiation,* 1996, Quorum
Humphreys, J., *Negotiating in the European Union*, 1997, Century Hutchinson
Schecter, J.L., *Russian Negotiating Behaviour*, 1998, United States Institute of Peace

## Negotiating

Lewicki, R. and others, *Negotiation*, 1998, McGraw-Hill
Pruitt, D.G., *Negotiation Behaviour*, 1982, Harcourt Brace*
Pruitt, D.G., *Negotiation in Social Conflict*, 1993, Open University Press

## Projects

Baguley, P., Teach Yourself Project Management, 1999, Hodder & Stoughton
Lock, D., Project Management, 6th edn, 1996, Gower

Meridith, J.R. and Mantel, S.J., Project Management – A Managerial Approach, 3rd edn, 1995, Wiley

## Relaxation

Craze, R., *Teach Yourself Relaxation*, 1998, Hodder & Stoughton

## Teams

Belbin, M.R., *Management Teams*, 1996, Butterworth-Heinemann.
Belbin, M.R., *Team Roles at Work*, 1996, Butterworth- Heinemann.
Katzenbach, J.R. and Smith D., *The Wisdom of Teams*, 1992, Harvard Business School Press

# Some useful web-sites

It is in the nature of the Web that sites are often transitory, here-today-gone-tomorrow creatures. Hopefully, the following are a little longer lasting:

policy.rutgers.edu/CNCR – Rutgers University Centre for Negotiation and Conflict Resolution
www.amazon.com or www.amazon.co.uk – Amazon web bookshop
www.audrie.com – US site giving, amongst other things, good advice on advertising and marketing your property
www.autobytel.co.uk – UK car buying and comparing site
www.AUTOMALLUSA.com – USA car buying and comparing site
www.bookshop.blackwell.co.uk – Blackwell's web bookshop
www. borders.com – Borders' web bookshop
www.canadr.com – Canadian International Institute of Applied Negotiation
www.clark.net/pub.diplonet – Home page for Diplonet network (designed to answer diplomats needs – including conflict resolution and negotiation)
www.conflictresolution.org/commandments – Ten Commandments for Negotiation, Mediation and Arbitration

www.excite.com – Search engine

www.hotbot.com – Another search engine

www.homesight.co.uk –Yellow Pages information site for people in UK housing market

www.igc.org – Institute for Global Communications – try Conflict Resolution page – lots of links

www.jibc.bc.ca/ccr – Centre for Conflict Resolution at Justice Institute of British Columbia

www.nova.edu/sss – see Alternative Dispute Resolution and web-sites link pages on School of Social and Systemic Studies at Nova South Eastern University (Florida)

www.pon.harvard.edu – Program on Negotiation inter-university study centre at Harvard University but involving Tufts, Harvard and MIT

www.topgear.beeb.com – BBC's *Top Gear* site – lots of impartial comments on cars

www.upmystreet.com – UK housing information site

www.which.net – UK Consumers Association web-site

# INDEX

**TEACH YOURSELF**

# PROJECT MANAGEMENT

## Phil Baguley

*Teach Yourself Project Management* is a practical introduction to the craft of project management. With diagrams, useful ideas, appropriate methods, checklists and tools, it explains and illustrates the what, why, when and how of this form of management. The ultimate guide for all who wish to develop the skills of effective project management.

The book shows you how to:

- manage, plan and organize your project from start to finish
- create an effective project team
- estimate and manage your project budgets
- solve problems, and monitor and control the activities of your project.

Phil Baguley is an experienced business writer and lecturer. He has held senior management roles in multinational corporations and worked as a management consultant in the UK and Europe.